ARE YOU ALWAYS UNDER THE GUN? IS THE CLOCK
A RELENTLESS MASTER—OR DOES TIME WORK FOR YOU?

Let Harold L. Taylor show you how to . . .

- Develop your own personal time policy
- Replace low priority tasks with meaningful ones
- Get on top of your paperwork—and stay there
- Run effective meetings
- Learn to delegate responsibility
- Apply invaluable time management techniques to your
  home and private life to make the most of your most
  priceless commodity—time

HAROLD L. TAYLOR has built a successful business
teaching people how to manage time. A prolific writer, he is
also president of Harold L. Taylor Enterprises, Ltd., a
multifaceted firm that publishes three magazines, manages a
variety of associations, and conducts the training programs
from which this book was derived. Here he details the time
management techniques he has developed to offer you
overwhelming success and life-changing results.

MAKING TIME
WORK FOR YOU

Harold L. Taylor

A DELL BOOK

Published by
Dell Publishing Co., Inc.
1 Dag Hammarskjold Plaza
New York, New York 10017

Dell ® TM 681510, Dell Publishing Co., Inc.

ISBN: 0-440-16260-2

Reprinted by arrangement with Beaufort Books, Inc.
Printed in the United States of America
First Dell printing—March 1983

INTRODUCTION

I assume you have already read at least one or two of the dozens of books that have been published on time management. I also assume, that after having read them, you are still unable to accomplish what you would like to accomplish in the time at your disposal. I think it's a safe assumption to make. Otherwise you wouldn't have picked up yet another book on time management.

What's the problem? Well, it may be that you're disorganized. If so, shaving an hour a day from your normal activities will not help one little bit because the activities will simply expand to fill the extra time you have available. Good old Parkinson's Law!

If that's the case, no seminar, course, or book will solve your problem. If you're disorganized to start with, you'll be disorganized afterwards. If you have sloppy, inconsistent work habits, a poorly laid out office, a cluttered work environment, inadequate file systems, then tips on time management will be of no avail. The few minutes shaved from telephone conversations, meetings or other activities won't mean a damn.

But if you will spend a few hours with me reading the

following pages and following the suggestions, you will be able to develop effective work habits, organize your office, files and methods, and streamline your workflow. In short, you will be able to get organized. *You will be able to manage yourself effectively with respect to time.*

And that's what it's all about. *Managing yourself.* Forget about other people. *They're* not your problem. *You're* your problem.

Read this book. Slowly. Try out the suggestions as they appear. They'll get you organized. Just as they've helped organize hundreds of others who have attended my seminars and workshops.

You may never have to read another book on time management.

But you'll have plenty of time to do so.

Read on.

CONTENTS

CHAPTER 1

DEVELOP A
TIME MANAGEMENT
PHILOSOPHY

The True Value Of Time

The value of time, like most commodities, is determined by supply and demand. If oil were in ample supply, it would not be as expensive. Similarly, water is considered almost worthless by most of us; but to someone lost in the desert, it is worth a fortune.

Time is the most valuable commodity of all. It is a non-renewable resource. And scientists will never be able to find a substitute. When our time is gone, we're gone.

Time seems to pass quickly for some, more slowly for others. For time is measured in past accomplishments. Those who look back and see few goals accomplished, few achievements, few times when they felt proud of what they have done—those people feel that life has sped by too quickly. They feel cheated.

But those who look back and are flooded with memory after memory of satisfying activities, achievements, relationships, feel they have lived a long and fruitful life.

For time is not seen as minutes, hours, or days. You

can't see intangibles that have no substance. Time is seen as events. Happenings. Experiences. It's seen as the glow on your children's faces when you tell them you are taking them to the zoo on Saturday. It's seen as the applauding crowd when you end your address to the home and school association. It's seen as the first cheque you receive for a short story submitted to a magazine. It's seen as that first promotion. It's seen as the pile of congratulatory cards when you graduate from college. Time is measured in events, not seconds. Squander time, and there will be fewer events to recall. Fewer accomplishments. Fewer moments of happiness.

Squander time, and you squander life.

If you are business-oriented you probably calculate time's value by determining your hourly rate, applying a percentage for overhead and emerging with a figure of, let's say, $32 per hour. Then you attempt to motivate yourself to stop wasting time by telling yourself that for each hour wasted you are throwing away $32. That's the way most time management experts approach it.

But it doesn't work. Because we're all spendthrifts. We know the value of money and yet we still squander it. After all, money can be replaced. Give us time and we will earn more.

There's the paradox. Time is *not* money. We need time to *earn* money. Time is *life*. We can use life for anything, but if it's all used up earning money, what else will there be to remember?

Do you want to spend the rest of your life earning money? Do you want your life to speed by with only memories of the activity of work? Or do you want to look back years from now and see the accomplishments, the achievements, the rewards?

If you do, you had better start managing your life —your time—right now. You won't get a second chance.

There's No Time To Manage Time

"I've just got to delegate more. I'm running like crazy from morning till night," confesses one manager. "But I just don't have the time to train anyone."

"I know we need written procedures," relates another. "Every time someone is sick, we're in a mess. But who has the time to sit down and write procedures? Certainly not me!"

"Sure, that's a great follow-up system. And I like the idea of a telephone and visitors log. That's fine if you've got the time to set it up!"

"I've finally made one of your time management seminars. This is the third time I've registered. Twice before I had to cancel out. I'm just too busy."

These are actual comments made at recent time management seminars. And they're typical.

We just don't have time to manage our time. And it's true. If we *did* have time to manage our time we'd have no need to manage it.

That's why most managers fail in their attempts to manage time. Because they are so busy, they grab at the little timesavers contained in books and articles: "How to cut 3 minutes off your telephone time" or "Ten ways to save time at meetings."

They shy away from the more complicated suggestions such as "get organized" or "delegate" or "design your own systems" because these are time consuming tasks in themselves. And time is one thing they haven't got.

Unfortunately, it is impossible to manage time. Time will be the same after we've left this earth as it was before we came. Time is unchangeable. Inflexible. Unyielding. No matter how you measure it, how you describe it, or how you use it, time cannot be influenced by any manager on this earth.

All we can ever hope to do is to *manage ourselves with respect to time.*

And to do this it does *not* take more time. It can't. Because there *is* no more time. It's all being used for other things. It's impossible *not* to use it, whether it be for sleeping, working, or daydreaming.

Whenever we want to perform some task that we are not presently doing, we have to displace other activities to make room for it. And therein lies the secret of what is referred to as *effective time management. To be effective we must displace less important tasks with more important ones.*

We can't wait until we have time to take on another task. We will never have any more time than we have right now. What we have to do is free up some of the time we have by eliminating non-productive or low priority activities and quickly replace them with more valuable activities.

Our effectiveness as managers is determined by the ratio of productive vs. non-productive activities filling the time at our disposal. And remember, *all* time is at our disposal.

Now take a look at those methods of managing ourselves with respect to time: the organized desk and work environment; the streamlined filing systems and follow-up files; the practice of delegation; the use of forms, logs, charts; the written procedures; the advance planning and scheduling of activities; and the dozens of sensible suggestions found in some of the time management books, articles, and seminars—the suggestions that you put off because you don't have the time.

Well you *have* the time. It's being utilized on activities which can be eliminated. *Believe* it. Everything you *do* can be eliminated. Some are vital to life and health so you won't want to eliminate them. Others are vital to your family and social life and you will not want to eliminate them.

But all the activities you do during your 8 or 9 hours at work *can* be eliminated (at least temporarily) without the world collapsing. Or even the business. If not, heaven help your business if you ever take a week's holiday, get sick for a few days, or get caught in a traffic jam one morning.

There is nothing more vital to your success as a manager than managing yourself effectively with respect to time. When you are managing yourself effectively, you are getting more accomplished. Not in less time. There's no such thing as more time or less time. But you are getting more things accomplished. *Meaningful things which move you closer to your personal and organizational goals.*

You don't have the time to manage your time? Well listen, you've got all the time there is to have. And the longer you procrastinate, the less you'll get out of life. So make a decision *now* to start managing yourself with respect to time.

What Is Important To You!

Before you can start eliminating and condensing the unimportant activities in your life, you must have a clear understanding of what the *important* activities are. *What is important to you?* What do you want to accomplish during your lifetime? You need to know. Because that's what time management (life management) is all about. The accomplishment of significant goals at the expense of those unimportant, time consuming activities.

If you've never thought about it before, now's the time to start. Plan your future. Visualize the type of person you want to be; what goals you want to achieve. Goals add purpose to life. They give us direction. Without them we drift, easy prey to the hundreds of time wasting activities that plague us all.

Your goals must be in writing. Don't kid yourself into believing that those nebulous thoughts about what you want to do next year or the year after are actually goals. They aren't. They're nebulous thoughts. Goals are in writing with completion dates and a plan of action for achieving them. They must be specific and measurable. Make sure your goals don't conflict with one another. It's unlikely you'll be able to save $10,000 and take a trip around the world in the same year. Make sure your goals are realistic.

Separate your goals into personal, family, and business goals. Here again, there should be no conflict. If you want to become president of the company, write a best-selling novel, and spend two hours every night with your family, there may indeed be conflict. Decide which goal is most important to you and give it priority.

For each goal, write down a list of steps necessary to

accomplish it. These steps will then become the activities you will use to replace the unimportant activities now being pursued.

Time management is a reachable goal for those who have the motivation. But you must see time as it really is —as a measure of your life. And you must know what you want to accomplish during your lifetime, the things that are really important to you. Then you will succeed for you will be able to displace those relatively unimportant activities with more meaningful activities— activities which lead you to your goals.

You can do it. Resolve now that you will respect every hour as a piece of your life. I will show you how to eliminate those activities that are unnecessary. And how to condense those activities that are necessary but unworthy of the slice of your life they are consuming.

Then *you* can use the resulting free time for meaningful activities that will lead you to your lifetime goals.

CHAPTER 2

GET RID OF
THE BACKLOG

Clean Up The Mess

You arrive at the office in time to be handed yet another bulging file of papers for approval. The stack of magazines on your credenza has grown higher. The 'phone messages on your spike have multiplied. Yesterday's unanswered mail is buried beneath the latest arrivals. Unfinished projects are barely visible beneath the clutter of memos, messages, and miscellaneous material. The phone rings. You pick it up, while gesturing to the two employees who have followed you into your office. They wait patiently with their problems while you hastily generate yet another scrap of paper while confirming to the caller that you will "look into it right away."

Hold everything! Hang up the 'phone, chase out those employees, and lock the office door. Don't risk ulcers or become another heart-attack statistic. Remember, it's your life you're wasting with these meaningless activities. Searching through piles of papers and hopping from crisis to crisis is not your bag. You have too much

respect for your time and too many goals that you want
to accomplish.

Your first step in making room for important activities
which will lead you to your goals is to get rid of the
backlog of paperwork and other obligations which pre-
cipitate interruptions and crises, and sap your energy.

Your priority task *right now* is to clear your desk and
in-basket. And to get organized. If you're not organized
—if you don't quickly stem the flow of excessive
communications—you'll be bogged down again in no
time. You have to start with the ruthless decision to
barricade your door, have your calls intercepted, and be
"out" to all visitors for a full day if necessary. If you feel
guilty about this due to all those urgent matters that need
attending to, reflect for a moment on what would happen
if you actually were out—with a bad case of ulcers, a
nervous breakdown, or worse. If you're still convinced
it's impossible, dedicate a Saturday or holiday to the
task. It's worth it.

Before you set up procedures which will keep you
organized, you have to clean up the mess. And this is no
time for neatness. Grab four envelope boxes. Mark them
"Magazines", "Junk Mail", "Routine", and "Priority".

Toss all magazines into one. Throw all junk mail into
another. Clear that desk. Low-priority items go into the
third carton marked "routine". Top-priority items go into
the last one. Don't waste too much time determining the
difference. If in doubt, it goes into the low-priority
carton. At this stage, consider priority items as only
those that must be completed within 3 days in order to
avoid some dire consequence. Within a half hour you
should have your desk and credenza tops completely
cleared. If it takes longer, you're actually reading the
paperwork or thinking about it, or setting especially

significant items aside. Don't fall into this trap or you'll sidetrack yourself to death.

It's a wonderful feeling to have a clear desk, but don't waste time contemplating it. Take that priority carton and start dispensing with the items one at a time. Don't pick from beneath the pile. Deal with the top item first, then the second and so on. Spend a good two hours on this top-priority carton. Some will be simple items requiring a hastily scribbled note of instruction to your secretary, a handwritten reply, or a simple "please handle" notation as you set it in the "outgoing" pile. Others will require 20 minutes or more of your time, several phone calls and some dictation. You may encounter an item near the top that takes you a full two hours of allotted time. But do it. Even if you don't complete it, you're two hours closer to having it completed.

When you've sorted your backlog of paperwork and spent at least 2 hours dispensing with priority items, it's time to plan a tentative schedule for the balance of the week—to be reviewed and changed later as you see fit. For the first week you may want to spend two hours each morning on that top-priority carton, moving to the low-priority one when it's completed. During this period have your secretary intercept your phone calls and visitors, and guard your closed door. If you have no secretary, at least close your door and deal with all interruptions as quickly as possible. Turn away visitors. Feign illness or play dead. But don't allow yourself to get sidetracked during that two hours each morning. To get organized properly you *must* start with a clear desk. The psychological lift it will give you will propel you through the subsequent stages of managing yourself with respect to time. After one or two weeks your entire backlog of work in those cartons will disappear. Your two hours in the morning can be devoted to going through those cartons of junk mail and magazines.

Don't spend much time on them. And don't be tempted to keep anything unless you can foresee a profitable use for it. Skim the magazines quickly. Photocopy any articles you may want to refer to later during leisure hours, and get rid of the magazines. Never thumb through pages twice. In Chapter 6 you will learn how to easily cope with a constant barrage of books, magazines, and reports; but in the meantime, just get rid of them quickly. Even if you have to pass them on or throw them out unread. Never let that desk get cluttered again. Whatever your scheduled time is for incoming mail, stick to it. Pick up each piece of paper only once. Scrap it. Delegate it. Answer it. But get rid of it. If it represents a ten-hour task, use the balance of your hour to get it underway. At the end of the hour, it goes into a "priority folder" for prime-time attention in the morning.

When your entire backlog of priority and routine items has disappeared, you can change your schedule. You'll find you have more time for planning and creativity the more organized you become.

Keep Your Desk Clear

Once your are rid of the backlog of work, you have to organize the flow of paperwork so it doesn't get ahead of you again. If someone opens your mail don't let them throw everything together. Have one folder for top-priority items, a second for routine matters, and a third for junk mail. (If you prefer, you can have your secretary screen the junk mail. Personally, I get a lot of good ideas from these unsolicited items, and like to browse through them quickly after completing my routine mail.) Have each folder a different color for easy identification. Magazines should be separate. Your mail should come to you with the top-priority file on top. And that's where you start.

If you can resist the overwhelming urge to peek beneath the piles, I guarantee you've got what it takes to manage yourself successfully.

If you cannot start on something because the information required hasn't arrived yet, or it's too soon to take action, get it off your desk and into a *follow-up file*.

All you need for a good follow-up file system are 31 manila folders for the days and 12 hanging files for the months, plus one hanging file for next year. Mark the front of the tabs on the manila folders with the days of the month from 1 to 31. Then color the backs of the tabs with a red magic-marker and number the backs as well. During your initial set-up, place the folders for the days which represent weekends and holidays in backwards. The red tabs will signal the holidays and you will not fall into the trap of scheduling follow-ups on those days.

Each day, at the time scheduled for your follow-ups, pull out the day's folder, dispense with the contents, and place the file in the hanging folder representing the next month. Repeat this procedure each day, turning the folders which represent the weekend (as well as any which represent statutory holidays or your vacation period) so they are in backwards with the red side exposed. Make use of them for following up on assignments, scheduling work, or planning projects. Follow-up files keep your desk clear of correspondence that can't be answered immediately. But don't use them as a storage place for paper you don't know what to do with. And don't use them as an aid to procrastination. Get in the habit of checking each day's file first thing in the morning and completing the follow-ups before your priority tasks are continued. After all, they're priority too or they shouldn't be in your follow-up file; they should be in the wastebasket. Utilize your follow-up files properly and they'll help keep you organized.

In addition to your follow-up files, make up a set of *project files*. Invariably there will be certain projects, meetings, events for which you will be accumulating material. Make up a file for each and color-code them with labels in addition to titles for quick identification and keep them in your desk drawer, credenza, or filing cabinet at your side. *But keep them off your desk.* Whenever something arrives in the mail that cannot be dispensed with immediately and involves one of these "projects," slip it into the appropriate file folder.

One of the necessities of keeping caught up (and keeping a clear desk) is to have a place for everything. Whenever correspondence, reports or other materials are received, don't allow them to remain in your in-basket or on top of your desk, credenza or table. Do one of the following right away:

(1) Scrap it
(2) Delegate it
(3) Do it
(4) Place it in follow-up file
(5) Place it in project file
(6) File it permanently

Never do it if you can scrap it or delegate it, and never file anything permanently unless it's vital that you refer to it again in the future.

For outgoing mail, set up a tier of outbaskets bearing the names of your subordinates. Anything you can possibly delegate should be sorted quickly and placed in these baskets with your instructions. Have your employees pick up their paperwork daily. Even your boss's memos don't have to be delivered if he or she is in the habit of dropping in a few times each day.

Guard your time carefully. It's your most valuable resource, so don't let others steal it. So far you've been able to clear up your backlog of paperwork, streamline the flow, keep a clear desk, and keep on top of current paperwork. You have forced yourself to work on priority items first, and all in all you feel a little better organized. But it's only temporary. Unless you set a daily time schedule—and stick to it—you'll be buried beneath paperwork again in no time.

In the next chapter, I'll show you how to develop a policy on time utilization which will *keep* your desk clear and prevent you from being victimized by external time bandits.

CHAPTER 3

DEVELOP A
TIME POLICY

Schedule A Quiet Hour

It's 8:45 A.M. and a cheery "good morning" echoes throughout the office as you make your way to your desk. You feel great. You *always* feel great first thing in the morning. You're what people refer to as a "morning person." Energy is at its peak from the time you swing out of bed at 7:00 A.M. until your enthusiasm takes a nose dive just before noon.

"Oh, say . . ." a voice follows you into your office, "could you approve these overtime slips and sign the payroll cheques when you get a minute?"

"Might as well get it over with now," you mutter in response, vaguely recalling a "do it now" principle expounded in a recent article on time management. "Hang on a minute, Alice."

Alice hangs on while you hastily scratch your signature on form after form. Alice gets tired of hanging on and disappears. Other shadows replace her. "Can I talk to you while you're signing those things?" one of the shadows asks. "I want to get your opinion on these new accounts."

"Sure, talk away," you offer, only half listening. Other shadows drop papers on your desk as you finish signing the cheques. The telephone rings. You hastily close the discussion on the new accounts as you reach for the 'phone. More visitors. The intercom. Morning mail. Your enthusiasm wanes. You decide on an early coffee break. But it's not that early. Nearly two hours have slipped away. "What a waste," you admonish yourself. "I haven't accomplished a thing yet and I have to leave in an hour for my luncheon appointment."

What a waste indeed. Not only have you not accomplished anything of consequence, but you have squandered the most valuable part of your day—your *prime time*.

If you are indeed a "morning person," you owe it to yourself to schedule your quiet hour during this early morning period. Close your door. Have 'phone calls and visitors intercepted. Don't schedule appointments or make outgoing calls during this quiet hour. Instead, spend the time and that abundance of energy working on your priority task: The task which will have the greatest impact on the accomplishment of your personal and organizational goals.

Many of us feel guilty about being inaccessible to our employees. We think it is our duty to be available at all times, to have an "open door policy."

And yet we would never think of allowing interruptions when we are in conference with our employees, clients, or customers. We view it as rude to talk on the telephone, receive visitors, or be inattentive in such situations.

If we don't feel guilty about respecting other peo-

ple's time, why should we feel guilty about respecting our own? We have just as much right (if not more) to hold meetings with *ourselves*. In fact we owe it both to ourselves and to our jobs. Only by scheduling interruption-free time each day can we maximize our effectiveness as managers.

Almost everyone will agree that they can get twice as much done in an hour of uninterrupted time (and do it better) than they can in two hours under normal office conditions. And no wonder. It is estimated that the average executive is interrupted every 8 minutes. How can we possibly be effective when we have to stop a job and reorient ourselves every 8 minutes!

This "quiet hour" should coincide with the time of the day when your energy level is at its peak. This may not be early morning. For some it's late morning or late afternoon. When you feel wide awake, refreshed, enthusiastic—that's the time you should schedule a meeting with yourself.

But don't waste this precious time by working on mundane tasks such as sorting mail or cleaning out a desk drawer. Utilize it for the tasks which are important, perhaps difficult. This could include planning, budgeting, working on a proposal for a new account or completing a major report which will affect you or your company's future.

If the hourly cost of your time works out to $25, then the hourly cost of your prime time will be closer to $50. You just don't spend $50 to straighten a desk drawer or open mail.

You also don't (or shouldn't) spend $50 to talk to a salesman, share a coffee with your peers, or review old times with your boss. So don't accept appointments or schedule meetings during your prime time.

Remember, it's more than money; it's part of your *life* that you're giving away.

If your prime time happens to be 8:30 A.M. to 10:00 A.M., then block that time out on your calendar. In advance. Draw a box around that time slot every day for the next few months. Label it "meeting" (with yourself) so you will not upset anyone.

Then, when anyone asks "Can I see you first thing Thursday morning?" you look at your calendar and reply, "Well, I have a meeting until 10:00 A.M. How about 10:00 or 10:30?"

Don't let meetings, visitors or appointments pre-empt your quiet hour. If you do, you are not managing your time effectively.

Admittedly, something will come up periodically that is even more important than the task you had scheduled for your quiet hour. If so, you have no choice but to pre-empt it. But this shouldn't happen very often.

And when it does, be aware of the cost. Car wash establishments, movie theaters, railways, airlines, all have additional charges for prime time. Unless you're a consultant you can't very well place a premium on *your* prime time. But why give it away? Keep it for yourself and increase your effectiveness.

Some managers claim it's impossible to reserve a quiet hour on a regular basis. They agree it would be terrific, but then go on to say that they have to answer their own 'phone, or they don't have a private office, or the boss keeps interrupting and "you can't tell the boss to get lost."

Admittedly, these are all problems. But most problems have solutions. If all else fails, spend your quiet hour in another office, a boardroom, or at home. And, as far as the boss is concerned, I haven't met the boss yet who was not interested in increasing the productivity of his or her staff. That is, once the boss realized that the purpose of the quiet hour was to increase effectiveness, not to hide from more work.

And effectiveness *will* increase, if you use your time wisely.

Your Time Policy

Since we'll never be able to get any more time than we already have, being effective becomes a matter of using our time wisely. It involves planning weeks and months ahead. It involves realistic estimates of how long each task will take. It involves self-discipline, concentration, and the power to resist distractions. And, above all, it involves developing a time policy. You have already carved out a period of time for a quiet hour. It's your *policy* to spend this prime time on priority work. But now you should formulate a time policy covering your entire day.

A time policy is a guide to be used in scheduling your tasks, appointments, meetings and other activities. It involves reserving certain periods of the day for specific activities. This makes you more effective in several ways. The habit (as it eventually becomes) of performing the same types of tasks at the same time each day reduces the brain's "start-up time"—the time it normally takes to get itself in gear and oriented to the task. It also allows you to make use of the natural breaks in a day (coffee breaks, lunch, quitting time) as deadlines to prevent jobs expanding to fill a greater time span (Parkinson's Law). This is particularly helpful in the case of meetings or appointments which tend to take twice as long as they should. And, of course, a time policy ensures that you use your prime time effectively —for priority tasks—leaving those routine activities for the afternoon doldrums.

I'm a "morning person" myself. I can get as much done before 10:00 A.M. as I can the rest of the day. Therefore, I guard this prime time jealously. If you don't make it a policy to utilize your prime time working on priority tasks, you'll find yourself scheduling appointments, meetings, or making calls during this most valuable part of your day.

If your prime time happens to be in the late afternoon or mid-morning, fine, then set your priority tasks and quiet hour to coincide with that particular time. Your policy should not be to accept phone calls, visitors, or work on routine tasks during this prime time.

Next, perhaps you would like to set a policy to hold all your staff meetings, interviews, counselling etc. late in the afternoon, let's say 4:00 to 5:00 P.M., as indicated on the time policy chart in exhibit 1. This would be a particularly good time to hold meetings since they tend to end a lot faster with 5:00 o'clock looming ahead. This would also be a good time to hand over all those assignments and tasks that you had dreamed up during the day. Resist the temptation to run back and forth between yourself and your employees handing out the assignments as they occur to you. Instead, jot down the tasks you would like to delegate and add to the list during the day. Then make one trip only—late in the afternoon. Interrupt your employees only once and you'll avoid wasting their time as well as your own.

Now you may want to set a policy of completing your routine tasks during the afternoon hours when your energy level has decreased and sluggishness has set in. This might be an excellent time to schedule visitors, return your telephone calls and work on those hundreds of "must do" items which do not require too much concentration or thought.

You may want to set a policy of having lunch sometime between 12:00 and 1:30 P.M. You may decide to utilize the time left over from this lunch hour to review your day's mail. Resist the temptation to work on your mail when it's received in the morning. Nothing is a greater waste of your prime time.

Important (but not priority) tasks, meetings, visitors, and calls could be handled just subsequent to your prime time in that space between 10:30 A.M. and 12:00 noon. Here again is an excellent time to hold meetings, receive visitors and return calls, since conversations proceed more quickly with lunch hour only minutes away.

Once you have drawn up your own personal time policy chart you should make your employees and associates aware of your policy concerning the scheduling of your time. Remember, this is only a policy. Policies are guidelines and can be changed if you have a very important visitor who insists upon seeing you in the morning (your boss, for instance). You may want to break your policy on occasion. But you will very quickly get into the habit of scheduling visitors, meetings, mail, magazines, etc. to fit your time policy chart.

Let's take a look at the sample chart reproduced in exhibit 1. This manager is in the habit of arriving about 8:45 A.M. His policy is to spend those 15 minutes getting his house in order. That is, going over a morning checklist which might include such items as photostating a schedule so that his key employees will know what his time commitments are. It could include checking his "idea" file in order to put some of them into action and a check of the follow-up file to determine which projects

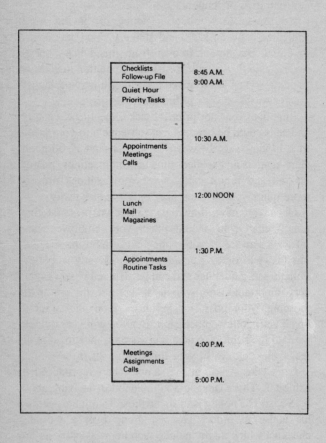

Checklists Follow-up File	8:45 A.M. 9:00 A.M.
Quiet Hour Priority Tasks	
	10:30 A.M.
Appointments Meetings Calls	
	12:00 NOON
Lunch Mail Magazines	
	1:30 P.M.
Appointments Routine Tasks	
	4:00 P.M.
Meetings Assignments Calls	
	5:00 P.M.

Exhibit 1 Time Policy Chart

or tasks are to be completed that day. Or the time might be spent simply reviewing the daily schedule and orienting himself to the tasks ahead.

Next comes his quiet hour between 9:00 A.M. and 10:30 A.M. during which priority tasks, which had been previously scheduled, are started. This is the prime time which must be protected from interruptions. His staff and business associates should be aware of the manager's unavailability during this time period. Calls should be screened and any essential interruptions kept to a minimum. This could be the most productive hour and a half of the manager's day.

From 10:30 A.M. to 12:00 noon, he may have several visitors scheduled. He could also return calls during this period, meet with fellow employees, or simply work on routine tasks. Or, if time permits, continue with those priority tasks.

He would then do his mail between 12:00 and 12:30 P.M. A little exercise, even though it might simply be a quick walk around the block, clears the cobwebs and increases efficiency during the afternoon. A light lunch should follow this exercise.

The next two hours or so would be spent dispensing with the bulk of those items on the "to do" list, making calls, completing projects, and in general working on those tasks which do not require much energy.

Finally, a meeting with his staff or a visit with some employees individually, developing assignments for the following day, rescheduling the tasks that are yet to be completed and planning the next day's schedule round out the afternoon.

You may have to experiment a little before formalizing your policy. Determine when you work best (your prime time) and when you feel sluggish. And review your scheduling policy every few months to see whether changing it might make you more effective.

If you have a secretary or assistant who makes your appointments for you, make sure he or she has a copy of your time policy chart. And don't allow deviations unless absolutely necessary. Give up your prime time grudgingly.

Time is the ultimate money since no money can be generated without the time spent to earn it. But you only have a limited amount of time to spend. So spend it wisely.

CHAPTER 4

SCHEDULE YOUR ACTIVITIES

"To Do" List Or Not "To Do" List

You're up to your elbows in a project that is taking longer than you thought and in the process of reaching for the phone to cancel a luncheon appointment, when one of your subordinates interrupts. "Got a minute?" he asks sheepishly.

Of course you've got a minute. In fact, you've got 360 minutes before you have to pack your briefcase and join the 5 o'clock migration. What can you say? You've already been interrupted, so you might as well say "Sure, what is it?"

So you say it. And you half listen while squirming stressfully, eyes darting between the phone and the report you had been writing. After a few painful minutes he finally leaves with his partially answered question. But you know he'll be back. They always come back.

"There just isn't enough time in the day," you mutter to yourself. Don't you believe it. If there were more hours in a day you would simply have to endure the same situations over a longer period of time.

There's no doubt you have a time problem. But the problem is not that you don't have enough time. It's how you're spending the time you've got.

You can't schedule your time. That's already done for you. There are 24 hours in every day, 4:00 P.M. occurs at the same time each day, and 8:00 P.M. always follows 7:00 P.M. But what you can and *should* do is to schedule your tasks. You must schedule your tasks in order to utilize your time effectively. And by scheduling I don't mean making a daily "to do" list. The practice of listing all the things you have to do and crossing them off as they're completed is better than nothing. Listing them in order of priority and working on the priority items first is a lot better. But the most effective method is to schedule the jobs directly into your planning calendar.

I admit that most time management authorities recommend that we spend time each morning (or the previous afternoon) writing a list of things to be done that day. But there's no way all those items could be done that day and, although authorities may claim that copying things over again "crystallizes our thinking," I believe it wastes our time. In fact, eventually we may convince our subconscious that the purpose of the exercise is to write out the jobs to be done rather than to do them.

I've seen managers with a lengthy list headed "Things to do Today" when "today" was taken up with all day meetings or seminars.

Jobs, projects, reports, appraisal reviews—all the priority items of a "to do" list—should be scheduled on your planning calendar along with the meetings, appointments, and luncheon dates. Combine your "to do" list with your planning calendar and you have an actual schedule—a commitment—of when you will perform each task. The real priority items of your "to do" list would appear this week on your calendar; the lower priority items might not appear for two or more weeks. But each task would be scheduled for a specific time on a specific day. If someone should ask if you're free for a meeting on Thursday afternoon at 3:00 P.M., the answer would be "no" if you had a report scheduled to be written at that time.

The routine tasks should be broken down into weekly "to do" lists and recorded directly in your planning calendar—but as a list to the right-hand side, not in any particular time frame. These are items you peck away at during spare moments. If you misjudge the number of items you can accomplish in a week, you will still have to copy some onto the next week's schedule.

But not many. For you have spread the items over several weeks. And hopefully you have allowed enough time for them. A good rule is to allow twice as much time as you think it will take for each task. This will compensate for those uncontrollable interruptions.

And keep interruptions to a minimum. Since you are now treating your priority jobs as though they were meetings or appointments, you are justified in closing the door until that particular scheduled task has been completed. Look upon it as an appointment with yourself.

The important thing is to schedule your tasks. So get a functional planning calendar, preferably with a week-at-a-glance or daily breakdown in half-hour units, and space for a weekly "to do" list. There are probably plenty on the market. Personally, I use a Quo Vadis Minister "Planning Diary" and it suits my needs perfectly.

How To Use Your Planning Calendar

Schedule personal and business items on your calendar.
If your son or daughter has a piano lesson or baseball
game scheduled one evening, mark it in your calendar.
Record hairdresser, doctor, and dentist appointments.
Parties and dances. Commitments to call friends. Everything that you don't want to forget. If they're so personal
you don't want your business associates to know about
them, enter them in code. But enter them. It will help
keep your life organized. And you will save time and
grief by not missing appointments or forgetting prom-
ises.

This is a *planning* calendar, not just a calendar to refer
to when you want to know what day it us. Use it to *plan*.
Block out chunks of time up to a year in advance. If you
have scheduled a quiet hour from 9:00 A.M. to 10:00
A.M., block out that time in advance with a highlighter
felt pen. Do it for the whole year—when you're waiting
in a doctor's office or watching T.V. Do the same for
vacations, business trips, seminars, meetings—anything
that you know in advance will occur during the year.
This will prevent you from inadvertently scheduling two
activities on the same day. And more important, it will
allow you to schedule *around* those activities.

Don't use more than one planning calendar. It's a
trap that most people fall into. They have a large desk
calendar plus a pocket-size calendar which they always
carry with them. The trouble is, they often look like they
belong to different people! Appointments, notes, remind-
ers jotted in the pocket calendar do not appear in the desk
calendar. And vice versa. And chances are it will happen
to *you* unless you can successfully condition yourself to

sit down every morning or evening and copy from one to the other to make them identical. And what a waste of time!

Use a planning calendar which is large enough for your purposes, but portable enough to carry in your briefcase or in a hefty purse. And take it with you wherever you go. There are odd times when you can't; a party or dance, a visit to the washroom, a shopping trip . . . , but on these occasions, you should have a few 3″ x 5″ index cards in your pocket. In fact you should always carry 3″ x 5″ index cards with you. They are excellent for jotting down ideas at the most unlikely times—while in a theater, jogging, or buying a hat.

Why don't you forget to copy from the index cards as well? Because they are exposed. Empty your pockets at night and the writing on those cards stares you in the face. You *have* to copy the notes into your calendar just to get rid of the awkward wrinkled things. But a pocket calendar is a closed container. There is nothing on the cover that tells you new appointments have been written inside—just as your kitchen cupboards conceal the fact that you're out of coffee or cereal. So get out of the habit of using two planning calendars.

Several people in my seminars claimed they kept *no* planning calendars. All the appointments, meetings, and activities were scheduled *for* them by their administrative assistants. If it works for them and they're happy with the way their time is being scheduled, I can't argue. But personally, I shudder at the thought of someone else scheduling *my life* for me. I insist upon having complete control of my time.

What I suggest you do is photostat your weekly planning calendar every Friday night or Monday morning and give a copy to your assistant or assistants *and*

your spouse. It's a real timesaver if they can tell business associates or friends on the 'phone the times you are or are not available without having to constantly check with you. It's not foolproof since you will inevitably be adding the odd appointment during the week. But, if you get in the habit of planning well in advance, chances are the current week will be pretty well locked up.

The Quo Vadis planning diary that I use also has a year at a glance for both the current and following years. I recommend you use it to schedule all meetings, seminars, vacations, conventions, and business trips that you know will occur during the year. It helps you plan effectively when you can see your busy periods and extended absences well in advance.

Another excellent way of keeping track of those important events and activities that will occur during the year is to invest in a large wall calendar. For example, one is produced by Hour Power Inc. of Crawfordville, Florida. It is 35″ x 45″, displays 15 months, and has ample space to mark in key activities.

A wall calendar of this type should be used if you have many meetings, conferences, business trips and other key events which everyone in the office should be aware of. Vacations can be scheduled on this chart so everyone can tell at a glance who will be away and when. Different types of activities should be color-coded for easy identification.

If you use a wall calendar, make sure that it is kept up to date by everyone whose activities appear on it. And periodically check it against your personal planning calendar to make sure there's not something on the wall

calendar that should be transferred to your personal
calendar.

If you find it impossible to keep the wall calendar
current, scrap it. It's better to have nothing than to have
something that misleads you.

CHAPTER 5

ORGANIZE YOUR OFFICE
AND YOURSELF

Engineer An Office Environment That Saves Time

Casinos in Las Vegas do an excellent job of engineering an environment that encourages you to *spend* time (and money). There are no clocks on the wall to remind you how late it is. Bright colors and airconditioning keep you awake. Conveniently located slot machines, plush seats, and free drinks make the spending of money painless. And the endless flow of "silver dollars" primes your gambling impulse.

Apply the Las Vegas concept to your own office. But design the environment in a way that encourages you and your employees to *save* time, not spend it.

Move your desk away from the doorway or you'll be distracted by everyone who passes by. It's an open invitation for people to catch your eye, wave, greet you —or worse still—drop in to say hello. A desk in view, combined with an open door policy, is deadly.

Arrange your furniture closely around you. You should be able to reach all your files, information, and office supplies without moving from your chair. Don't fall into the trap of arranging your office as though it were your living room at home. It isn't. The name of the game is "results," not "comfort." Have a separate area or room for relaxing, entertaining or impressing. But your desk area is your work area, and everything should be arranged accordingly.

At the time of writing, my office was arranged in a particular way. It's probably different now, since I keep experimenting with slight changes. No office layout is sacred. Experiment. Find out what arrangement suits you best.

Many of my business associates kid me by asking, "How do you get into your work area—climb over your desk?"

"Well, not quite," I usually reply. "But it is difficult to get out once I get in." It's true. You'll notice I have to walk the long way around my desk to get in and out (and a tight squeeze at that) which doesn't seem to conform to time management principles. But the very fact that it's difficult to get out discourages me from running back and forth between my office and those of my employees. Or getting coffee. Or rushing out to greet friendly voices. I'm at my work station to work. To get results. I'll wait until the end of the morning or afternoon before bothering my employees with accumulated queries and assignments unless they come to me.

But that shouldn't happen too often if I've delegated properly, trained properly, and encouraged time management on the part of my employees.

My desk is not as clear as it looks. It is never entirely clear. But my objective is to have only three things on my desk at one time (in addition to the telephone): my day-planner, my daily "telephone and visitors log" (to be discussed shortly), and the project or correspondence I am working on at that moment.

Don't leave piles of paperwork on your desk—not even if you plan to get it all finished during the day. It's not only messy and space consuming, it is also distracting. Unfinished work tends to divert our attention, makes us feel weary, and lowers our effectiveness. Follow the suggestions in Chapter 2. Set up project files and follow-up files. Keep them in your right-hand drawer or in a cabinet at your side. Your in-basket should be empty once you've dispensed with your mail. Your wastebasket ideally should go between your in-basket and out-baskets (delegation trays). This makes it easy to scrap material that comes in, before passing most of the remaining paperwork to your delegation trays. This wasn't possible in my case since it would have interfered with the file drawers.

Keep your articles and information binders in a bookcase or credenza behind you. The preparation of this library of facts will be discussed in the next chapter.

Your briefcase should be open and within reach. Toss in magazine articles and reports that can be used as fillers for those unavoidable waiting periods that crop up later.

Make sure you have all the equipment you need to work effectively without interruption. Have your own 3-hole punch, scissors, glue, labels, and file folders. Don't pinch pennies and try to share inexpensive equipment with the rest of the office. Your time is more valuable. If you use something on a regular basis, buy one for your office and save yourself dozens of trips (and searches).

Have a spot for everything and don't vary it. Know exactly where to reach for your telephone, dictation unit, dayplanner, paperclips, staples, and pens.

Take advantage of "gadgets." Any office equipment or gadgets that will save you time are worth considering. A telephone shoulder-rest allows you to sign cheques and perform routine tasks while talking. Touchtone telephones save precious time in dialing. An intercom system cuts down on interoffice travel and idle time. An electronic reminder prevents you from spending too much time on low priority tasks or meetings. "Memory" typewriters produce accurate letters fast. Pocket calculators, recorders, delegation trays, forms, and checklists all help to conserve that precious commodity, time. Investigate their use. If they help keep you organized, they're worth ten times their cost.

Buy a cassette recorder. If you're now writing a lot of letters by hand, it will pay for itself within a few months. You can dictate four times as fast as you can write. It enables you to utilize travel time and waiting time. Your secretary doesn't have to decipher your writing and it won't add to his or her paper overload.

Develop a workable filing system. File daily and throw out daily. Don't allow papers to accumulate. Keep only those that are absolutely necessary. Staple papers together; don't use paperclips. File correspondence according to date, with the most recent at the front. Color-code the folders. Design the system to suit your own requirements. But remember, files that just grow are not systems; systems are planned.

It's difficult to manage your time and organize your thoughts when you have a disorganized office, desk, and filing system. So organize an office and system that will work for *you*.

Although the main concern of this book is to help you manage *yourself* with respect to time you, as a manager, have an equal responsibility to see that your employees manage themselves with respect to time. So review the main office layout as well. Does the arrangement of desks, files, and cabinets match the work flow? Supplies and equipment should be near the people who use them.

Employees who frequently deal with one another should be located in the same area. Consider movable files, storage devices, and area dividers. Remember, if one employee wastes 15 minutes a day looking for supplies or running back and forth between desks, that's two weeks of lost time per year. So make sure the main office is organized.

Get Organized

"Do you have the cost on that word processor yet?" the voice on the line asks impatiently.

"Oh yes, Sam," you reply, digging through a pile of messages. "Bill gave me the figures over the 'phone earlier today." Now where's that scrap of paper, you grumble to yourself. It was here a minute ago. There's an awkward pause, some time-killing small talk, then an embarrassing delay as you can't seem to locate the figures.

"Well look, just give me Bill's number, and I'll check it myself," the frustrated voice snaps in your ear.

"Maybe that's just as well," you agree. "He was discussing some options that only you could pass judgment on. . . ."

You rush to rationalize the inconvenience you have caused while trying to recall where you put Bill's number. Then you do recall. You never recorded it. Bill had initiated the call, you were busy at the time, and it just hadn't occurred to you to ask for it.

"I'm afraid I don't seem to have his number anywhere," you eventually tell him. Sam makes some remark to the effect that he'll look it up in the 'phone book and mercifully hangs up.

"Oh boy," you sigh. "If I could only develop a system that automatically records all calls, notes all 'phone numbers, summarizes the significant points from any conversation and highlights all the follow-ups required."

You *can* develop such a system. And regardless of how conscientiously you apply time management strategies discussed in books and articles, unless you *do* develop effective systems, you won't be able to avoid situations like the one described above.

Develop a daily organizer. It doesn't matter whether you call it an organizer, workbook, daily log or planning binder. It's what it does for you that counts. I've developed what I call a "planning binder" which has become my indispensable time management tool. It's a large three-ring binder containing eight sections. It's my daily diary that records everything as it occurs and keeps me posted as to what has yet to be done. Design one that suits your own needs. You should never experience misplaced messages or telephone numbers. Or follow-ups that have slipped your memory. Here are three sections you should definitely include:

1. *Daily telephone and visitors log.*

This section eliminates the need for those scraps of paper which keep getting misplaced. And it prevents you from ever having to rely on your memory after a visitor has left or a caller has hung up. It consists of a series of simple forms on which you record the caller's name, company, nature of business discussed and any follow-ups required. The follow-up section is to the right of the form where it stands out. When the follow-up is completed, a cross is put over that section. By flipping

through the pages you can tell at a glance whether any
follow-ups are required. It's a permanent record of any
call or visit made or received, and the sheets can
eventually be filed away as a diary, or discarded once
any relevant information, such as telephone numbers,
has been lifted. It takes only a few seconds to fill out
—the same amount of time it takes to scribble on those
scraps of paper that get misplaced—but it saves hours.

Try it. Keep the forms in a binder on your desk. Have
it open at the day's date ready for action. When you
make or receive a call, automatically set the binder in
front of you and, instead of doodling on a scrap of paper
as you talk, make notes in the "Nature of business" area.
When the person at the other end of the line makes a
request, jot it down in the "Action Required" area. Write
in the name and company of the caller at the start or
during a pause in the conversation. Before you hang up,
be sure to get the 'phone number, even if you have it in
your directory. It only takes a second for the person to
give it; it could take ten times that long for you to look it
up.

You now have the best back-up in the world. You can
relate who called, when, about what, and the nature of
the action requested—even months later. Can your
memory do that? If requests or even the 'phone calls
have ever slipped your mind this is not only a timesaver,
it is a *must*.

The same procedure is followed when someone drops
into your office (by invitation, hopefully). Making a note
of the request can only impress the visitor with your
obvious intention of following it up.

This all sounds very easy. It's not. You find you
"forget" to use the log. Or it gets put away somewhere.
Or it's not opened and you can't be bothered going

through the hassle of recording what will probably be a brief call. It takes persistence. Force yourself to use it for a week. The second week it will become easier. After that, it will become a habit.

2. *Delegation record.*

Ever assign a task or project to someone and then forget to follow it up? Then add another series of sheets to that binder. Simple forms that indicate the task, to whom you have delegated it, the due date, and actual completion date. It's surprising how promptly people get things done when they know you're recording it. Whenever assigning a task, mutually agree on a completion date and record it. Keep a separate sheet for each supervisor reporting to you. It not only prevents you from forgetting, it becomes a permanent record of your employees' performance. Compare the "due date" with the actual "date completed." Write remarks in the "Comments" column. Was the task performed effectively? Was it complete? This becomes a handy reference during performance appraisal time.

It also stops you from inadvertently piling all the jobs onto one person. A long list of assignments for Joe and very few for John will stand out on this form over a period of time.

3. *Telephone directory.*

No need to fumble for your little black book whenever you want to make a call. Just add another section with alphabetical dividers, make up your own name and address forms, and you have your own directory. It's constantly at your fingertips. And the forms can have room for other essential information such as who the person is, the circumstances of your meeting, his physical description and so on. Nothing's more frustrating than seeing names in your directory a few years later, and wondering who they are. Your directory never fills up or becomes outdated. Simply add or remove pages at will.

You can add other sections to suit your needs. My planning binder also contains a section for controls (charts and graphs from financial statements), a monthly plan of projects, personal time sheets, checklists, and personal goals. Oh yes, and plenty of blank paper. There's no need to have any scratch pads, notes or correspondence on your desk. Just this binder and the project you're working on at the time.

Are you starting to feel a little more organized now? If not, you've moved too quickly. Reread these first chapters. Take advantage of anything you feel will help you. Then put them into effect. The subsequent chapters will add icing to the cake. You will be able to refine your work habits and methods to increase your effectiveness even more. You will soon be managing yourself effectively with respect to time.

CHAPTER 6

CONTROL THE
INFORMATION
EXPLOSION

Build Your Own Reference Library

"As a matter of fact, Bill, I *just read* an article on profit sharing only a few months ago." You try to recall the magazine. "I'm sure I kept it," you continue, " 'cause I knew we'd be considering a similar plan someday."

"What magazine was it?" Bill asks. "I'm anxious to take a look at it."

"I'm trying to remember." You pause. "I'm sure it was either *Canadian Business* or *Executive*. Not too long ago." You pause again. "Tell you what. I'll check the issues and get back to you. I'm sure I can find it."

"Great, I'd appreciate it. How about sending me a copy of the article when you find it?"

"Sure thing, Bill. I know I've still got it. I keep all magazines that have information we could use someday. Shouldn't take long."

Well if it takes you only 2 minutes, that's 1 minute and 30 seconds too long. And chances are it'll take a lot longer than that. By the time you retrieve and flip through 3 or 4 issues of 2 or 3 magazines, you've sacrificed another small slice of your life in needless activity.

There's a way to cope with the information explosion that is upon us. But you must have a system.

Chances are you are doing more reading related to your business than ever before. Magazines, journals, business papers, and conference proceedings, flow steadily to your desk. Tens of thousands of new books are published each year. Daily newspapers bombard you with 3 or 4 million words a week.

And the information explosion has only just begun. At the rate at which knowledge is growing it is estimated that in 50 years time, today's knowledge will account for only 3 percent of the total knowledge available at that time. How can you cope with all this information?

Well, before you rush off to take a speedreading course, remember that effective reading involves knowing what to read as well as *how* to read it. The first step is to establish some method of screening the chaff from the wheat and spending your valuable time on only those magazines and books which will help you reach your business and personal goals.

I've been conducting a survey among the managers in my seminars. Results indicate that managers spend an average of 13 hours each week reading business-related material. The largest chunk of this time is spent reading business and trade publications. These magazines are an obvious source of valuable information. But they are also making increasing demands on your time. Here is one method of coping with them:

1. If a magazine is not providing information that you can use, cancel your subscription or get off the

mailing list. There's no such thing as a free magazine. Our time is anything but *free*.

2. When you receive a publication, resist the
impulse to toss it aside. That kind of procrastination
often builds mountains of magazines which end up
being bulldozed to a shelf or table or trucked to
another executive's desk unread. It takes only a few
minutes to glance at the title page or skim the
articles to determine which ones will be relevant to
your area of interest. So when you've finished your
priority mail and are working on the routine,
dispense with the magazines as well.

3. If you're the only one who sees the magazine, rip
out those articles you've selected and scrap the rest.
More than likely though, you'll want to circulate
the magazines or in the case of good reference
magazines, retain them in your library. In that case
have someone photocopy the articles you want to
read and retain.

good

4. File the selected articles in 3-ring binders,
appropriately identified. For example, all articles
dealing with time management would be placed in
one binder, those on sales meetings in another, and
so on. Color-code the label you use on the spine.
Better still, use a cartoon or symbol for easy
identification. My "time management" binders have
clocks on them, "communications" have phones,
"meetings" has a boardroom scene and so on. This
way I'm able to select the right binder instantly.

cute

5. Now you can leave the actual *reading* to a
scheduled time period. Try to take advantage of idle
time by reading during business trips, while waiting
in doctors' offices and airports, or during periods of
relaxation. Read with a highlighter pen, marking

relevant paragraphs and sentences. Make notes in the margin. This becomes your permanent reference library and rereading articles to find the relevant parts will not be necessary.

Books should also be read with a highlighter and marked up as you read. Significant pages can be copied or even summarized for inclusion in your reference binders. The same thing goes for newsletters, conference proceedings, and other literature. Anything worth reading is worth retaining for future reference—but only those significant parts. If you read a lot of library books, hold off on that yellow marker and marginal notes. You know exactly where you can get that book again if you need to refer to it. Fill out a form similar to the one shown in for every library or "borrowed" book you read. File the form in the appropriate binder.

Speedreading courses have been known to increase reading ability from 200 words per minute to over 800 words per minute without decreasing comprehension. If you feel you could benefit from such a course, by all means take it. But not until you have organized yourself in a manner which allows you to retain the information you read.

Most people are overly concerned about their reading speed. It's important. But it's nothing compared to the importance of retaining all the significant information in an organized manner for easy retrieval in the future. We forget at least 75 percent of what we read in only 3 months. Assuming you have a superior memory and never forget more than 75 percent, and you read an average of 13 hours each week, *then you are forgetting what you spent nearly 10 hours doing.* What a flagrant waste of precious time—and life!

Read With A Purpose

If you're going to read hundreds of books, articles and reports each year to keep current with your profession, you must read with a purpose.

This involves *active* reading. Search for information and answers as you read. Skip words and grasp ideas. If the title of the article is "Pitfalls of Flexible Hour Systems," look for those pitfalls and highlight them with a felt pen. If you read an article titled "Piecework Pays Off," search for the reasons piecework pays off. Be aware of what you're looking for. Don't be passive. Don't be afraid to skip words, sentences—even paragraphs. Your time is valuable. You're not obligated to read everything the author writes. You're obligated to obtain the information you *need.*

It isn't necessary to take a speedreading course to speed up your reading. Through effort and practice you can double your speed. And retain more. *But be an active reader.*

Don't Junk "Junk" Mail

If you've been discarding all unsolicited mail without looking at it, great. That's what I'd recommend until you're organized and can afford a few luxuries.

But by now you should be better organized. And you can get many good ideas from this junk mail. In addition, it keeps you up to date on new products, seminars, and services available.

If you have a secretary or receptionist you should be receiving your mail in four folders marked priority, routine, magazines, and junk mail. And I recommend you review them in this order.

You should also have an "idea" file. When you find something of interest while quickly sifting through the junk mail, drop it in the "idea" file. But before you do, note on the piece of literature the reason you are keeping it. A month later you may forget why you did. The idea will have escaped you.

Make it a habit at the first of each month to review this "idea" file. Throw out the material if you feel you may never implement the idea it represents. Put other ideas into action. If something has remained in your "idea" file for over three months—and you've passed over it twice —it should probably be thrown out. Don't be a pack rat. Keep all your files lean.

Make sure *you* control the information explosion; don't let *it* control you.

CHAPTER 7

GET CONTROL
OF YOURSELF

Recognize Your Major Timewaster

Ask people what their major timewaster is and most of them will lead you to believe it is *other people*. "Constant interruptions," they'll tell you; "Employees constantly making mistakes"; or, "All those damn meetings I have to attend."

Don't you believe it. *We* are the ones primarily responsible for our own time management problems. And if you're going to be successful in managing yourself with respect to time, you will have to accept that fact—and do something about it.

Exhibit 2 lists all the timewasters that are entirely or partially within your control. Doesn't leave much, does it? And I guarantee that if you reduce the timewasters that are within your control, the other ones will be unable to curb your effectiveness.

Most of them will be eliminated by proper organization, systems, procedures, and self-discipline. But a few involve breaking bad habits which you have acquired over the years. The two habits which constantly plague

PINPOINT YOUR TIME WASTERS

The first step in effective time management is to recognize that we are the ones primarily responsible for our own time problems — not the other people. By managing ourselves more effectively with respect to time, we can greatly increase our accomplishments within a given time frame.

If you are not satisfied with what you are now able to accomplish in the time available, determine which of the following time wasters are applicable to yourself. They are all within your control.

Once you have pinpointed those time wasters which seem to apply to your situation, set up a plan to systematically reduce their effect.

- ☐ LACK OF DELEGATION
- ☐ PROCRASTINATION
- ☐ LACK OF PLANNING, SCHEDULING, ORGANIZATION
- ☐ TROUBLE GETTING STARTED IN MORNINGS
- ☐ OVER-EXTENDED COFFEE BREAKS & LUNCHES
- ☐ IDLE TIME, TALK, DAYDREAMING
- ☐ SORTING & DISPENSING WITH MAIL
- ☐ SEARCHING FOR FILES, INFORMATION
- ☐ READING MAGAZINES, JUNK MAIL
- ☐ SHUFFLING PAPERS
- ☐ PROOFREADING AND SIGNING LETTERS
- ☐ CONSTANT CHECKING ON EMPLOYEES
- ☐ SPENDING TIME ON NON-PRIORITY ITEMS
- ☐ INTER-OFFICE TRAVEL
- ☐ TOO LONG ON TELEPHONE
- ☐ RE-WRITING MEMOS & LETTERS
- ☐ MARTINI LUNCHES
- ☐ LACK OF WRITTEN GOALS
- ☐ INABILITY TO SAY "NO"
- ☐ HOLDING UNNECESSARY MEETINGS
- ☐ POOR CONTROL OF MEETINGS
- ☐ RELYING ON MENTAL NOTES
- ☐ DELAYING DISTASTEFUL TASKS
- ☐ NO "QUIET HOUR"
- ☐ NOT USING PRIME TIME FOR PRIORITY WORK
- ☐ NOT UTILIZING WAITING TIME AND TRAVEL TIME
- ☐ FILING TOO MUCH, THROWING OUT TOO LITTLE

Exhibit 2 Pinpoint Your Time Wasters

- SELF-INTERRUPTIONS
- NOT UTILIZING FORMS
- INDECISION
- ALLOWING CONSTANT INTERRUPTIONS BY OTHERS
- WRITING INSTEAD OF PHONING
- INEFFICIENT OFFICE LAYOUT
- INSISTING ON KNOWING ALL AND SEEING ALL
- NOT KEEPING SECRETARY/ASSISTANT ADVISED OF APPOINTMENTS, MEETINGS
- NOT HAVING FACTS, TELEPHONE NUMBERS, AT HAND
- UNCLEAR COMMUNICATIONS
- NOT TAKING ADVANTAGE OF TIME-SAVING GADGETS
- TOO MUCH ATTENTION TO DETAIL, PERFECTIONISM
- NO DAILY PLAN
- NO SELF-IMPOSED DEADLINES
- LEAVING TASKS UNFINISHED & STARTING NEW ONES
- ALLOWING UPWARD DELEGATION
- DOING OTHER PEOPLE'S WORK
- NOT EFFECTIVELY TRAINING STAFF
- FIREFIGHTING
- PREOCCUPATION WITH PROBLEMS
- NO FOLLOW-UP SYSTEM
- NOT ACTIVELY LISTENING
- TOO MUCH TIME ON PERSONAL & OUTSIDE ACTIVITIES
- POOR ATTITUDE TOWARD THE JOB
- WORRY, LACK OF CONFIDENCE
- LACK OF PROCEDURES
- FAILURE TO USE DICTATION EQUIPMENT
- POOR WRITING SKILLS
- ABSENTMINDEDNESS

managers—procrastination and absentmindedness—will be dealt with in this chapter.

Kick The Procrastination Habit

Whoever said "Procrastination is the thief of time" sure knew what he was talking about. It robs us of valuable time, keeps us disorganized, and leads to interruptions, crises, and stress.

Once we get hooked on procrastination, we find plenty of ways to support the habit. It's fed by the many excuses for delay such as shuffling paperwork, straightening our desk, sorting through the mail or engaging in idle conversation.

Procrastination is a parasite, eating away at our effectiveness as managers. We must understand why and how it operates and eliminate it.

Most of us tend to procrastinate if the job is a big one. We kid ourselves into thinking we'll have a larger block of time available at a later date. But we never do, unless we actually schedule that block of time, as discussed in Chapter 4. Many tasks don't have to be put off at all. If they don't require a lot of set-up or make-ready time, they can be completed gradually, a little at a time. The trick is to start the task regardless of whether we have 5 minutes or 5 hours. At least we can bring the task 5 minutes closer to completion.

Time management authority Alan Lakein refers to this as the "Swiss cheese" method—making small holes in an overwhelming task until it looks like a Swiss cheese and is finally eliminated altogether. There's no such thing as an insurmountable task—only long links of small tasks that collectively seem insurmountable.

We never wallpaper a whole room. We paper one strip

at a time, one wall at a time, until the whole room is papered. Similarly, we don't write a book. That's an overwhelming task. We simply write series of paragraphs which link together to form a chapter, which in turn link with other chapters to form a book. We must approach many large tasks this way or we will never get the courage to tackle them at all. We'll procrastinate.

For proof that the above approach really works, take a look at the many activities you *don't want* to end. Our lives, for instance, are used up only too quickly—one year at a time, one day at a time, one hour at a time. Yet how insignificant that one hour seems in relation to a lifetime.

Try it. If you want to move three hundred files from your office to your home, simply throw 3 or 4 into your briefcase each night. Within a few months you will have moved them all. If you have to write something involving a long, involved procedure, simply spend 10 minutes each day writing one step in that procedure. If you have to clean out a closet at home, tackle only one hanger or one carton each night.

Don't let overwhelming tasks force you to procrastinate. This was brought home to me when I was a high school graduate working in a supermarket. My older brother urged me to continue my education by getting a university degree in the evenings. When I protested that I didn't have the time or the money for such an undertaking, he suggested I take only one course per year. "But that's impossible!" I exclaimed. "At that rate it would take me 15 years. I'd be 33 years old before I got my degree!" He was unimpressed. "Well, you'll be 33 years old anyway," he replied.

How right he was. I didn't take his advice and 15 years later found myself 33 years old, but *without* a degree. Time passes regardless, so why not go after your goals while it does.

We tend to postpone jobs that are unpleasant. If we have to deny a request, cancel an order, or dismiss an employee, we drag our feet. And why not? It's distasteful. So we worry about it. We get upset. Feel the stress. Oh, how we loathe the time when we cannot postpone it any longer and finally have to act. But act we must, and when we finally do—what a relief! A load has been lifted from us.

Why suffer by dragging out the inevitable? Get the "do it now" habit. Don't tell yourself, "It's unpleasant, so I'll delay action." Say instead, "It's unpleasant, so I'll *do it now* and get it over with." Your effectiveness will increase because an unpleasant task isn't hanging over your head. You won't be under stress. And your prompt action may prevent further complications or embarrassment, squelch rumors, and improve relationships. Replace the procrastination habit with the "do it now" habit.

Although reluctance to start unpleasant or time consuming tasks is the major cause of procrastination, some managers are simply disorganized. They lack clear-cut goals, don't plan or schedule adequately, have misplaced priorities and manage themselves poorly with respect to time. The procrastination parasite thrives on these individuals. They are so busy hopping from one job to another and dealing with constant interruptions that they postpone everything that isn't yet a crisis.

If you were a victim of disorganization, the earlier chapters should have helped you. Have your goals in writing. Plan your months, days, and hours. Reject activities that won't lead you closer to your goals and schedule the others in order of priority. Make appointments with yourself to start each project at a particular time, and keep those appointments. Schedule those long or distasteful activities early in the day. Then get a head start by starting early. A fast and productive start sets the stage for a productive day. Practice self-discipline. Make up your mind *now* that you are going to adopt a "do it now" attitude.

Overcome Absentmindedness

Ever find yourself staring blankly into a filing cabinet drawer wondering what it is you were looking for? Or trying to recall where you put your spare pair of eyeglasses? Or searching in vain for your misplaced car keys? If so, you're no different from the rest of us; next to forgetting names, absentmindedness is the most common complaint of managers attending my memory-training seminars. It is a time consuming habit that must be overcome. And it *can* be overcome. But it requires a conscious effort. Even persons with excellent memories can be absentminded, for absentmindedness is nothing more than inattention. If you were not preoccupied with other thoughts and paid attention to where you put your spare pair of glasses, you would remember where they were.

We must educate ourselves to do things consciously and not allow our thoughts to wander. The first step is to make up our minds right now that we are going to make the effort. We must convince ourselves that we *want* to recall where we left things and that we *are* going to recall where we left them. Then we can assist our ability to recall by making sure we have a vivid picture of where we put things.

This can be done in several ways. One is to have a

reason for putting something where you do. Did you put your glasses in the top left-hand drawer of the kitchen cupboard because it's the closest one to the front door? Or in the medicine cabinet because that's where you keep your spare razor batteries, shoelaces, etc.? If you have a logical reason for putting things where you do, you will probably be able to recall the *reason*—which in turn will remind you of the *place*.

Another way is to say it aloud. "I am putting the spare office keys in the top drawer of my desk because that's where the deposit-box key is kept." Your brain listens to and remembers the sound of your voice.

To reinforce it even further, make a conscious association between the object and the place where you're putting it. For example, visualize that top drawer slamming shut on your glasses, smashing them into a thousand pieces. Get action into your picture. Exaggerate. The more ridiculous, violent, and colorful visualizations are hard *not* to recall.

The very idea of making an association makes you think of what you're doing for at least a fraction of a second and that's usually all that's necessary. Remember, the eyes cannot see when the mind is absent.

Memory lapses sometimes result from concentrating too much on one thing and not enough on another. When we're thinking about that important visitor, catching a plane, or giving a speech, we tend to forget the habitual things we do such as removing our eyeglasses and setting them on top of the filing cabinet or bookcase. But with a little willpower, we can get into the habit of making split-second associations.

If you bring a report with you when you go to lunch, and then set it on the chair, you can make sure you won't forget it by associating it with the check. Visualize the check with a report written on it in glaring red phosphorescent ink. Or visualize a huge report nailed across the exit blocking your way.

This may all sound ridiculous—it is. And that's why it works. And in time you will find you have acquired the habit of *thinking about what you are doing.*

There's no easy way of curing absentmindedness. For it requires continuing attempts to be aware of what we are doing, of where we are putting things, of things we are supposed to do, or of calls we are supposed to make. It's so easy to park the car and rush into the mall without paying one bit of attention to where we parked the car. It's easy because our mind is on our shopping or our time problem and not on the parking spot. Once we have acquired the habit of automatically picking out some landmark—a lamppost or flagpole for instance—and noting where our car is in relationship to it, it becomes easy to remember. Once we *consciously* make an association, it's easy to recall it later.

An organized person is usually better at remembering. And right now you should be pretty well organized.

But remember, always make an effort to concentrate on what you are doing.

CHAPTER 8

DELEGATE
FOR RESULTS

Your Time Cube

Now comes the crunch. The previous chapters were designed to get you and your surroundings organized. By doing so, you will have reduced the time spent on routine activities without causing any additional stress. The resulting free time *must be spent* on important tasks. It's one thing having an organized desk, files, systems, and work habits. Utilizing these tools to accomplish meaningful tasks is something else.

In Chapter One I emphasized the fact that we only have 24 hours in each day. No more, no less. And that in order to achieve meaningful goals and be effective as managers we must displace many of the meaningless or less important activities with priority, results-oriented activities.

Now I will show you how you can work more effectively by making better use of your time. Rather than extend your workday to 10 or 12 hours, you will be able to *reduce* the time spent at work if this is your desire.

The sadness of it all is that many people do try to extend their working day in order to get more done. And it's futile. As Parkinson's Law so aptly states, work expands to fill the time available for it. Work is not solid. It is like a gas—hundreds of particles called "activities" which expand to fill the extra space.

That's the reason time management experts urge us not to work longer hours in an attempt to cure our time problem. Not only does it interfere with our family and social life, it makes us less effective because we then look upon our evenings as an extension of our day. If we run out of time while working on a project, we simply shrug and tell ourselves we'll finish it in the evening. We do this rather than utilize that fifteen minutes before normal quitting time, rather than do a "less than perfect" job, or rather than rush, put ourselves under pressure, or impose on someone else. *Rather than do something about our problem of having too many activities to complete in a normal work day.*

An alternative is to allocate a specific number of hours and finish your tasks during that period of time, come hell or high water. The problem with this "solution" is that not only will hell and high water come, so will stress, and possibly nervous disorders, ulcers or a heart attack. You can only compress activities into so much space. A gas can be compressed. But the more it is compressed, the greater the pressure exerted on the walls of the container.

This is what causes stress, breakdowns or worse. People put themselves under extreme pressure by cramming more and more activities into the same time container. Until, finally, the pressure becomes so great that the container explodes.

You might say, "Well I'd rather extend my day than

explode!" But extending your day only delays the inevitable. If you have a larger container of time, you can cram more activities into it. And you will. It's our nature. And when the explosion finally comes you'll probably be the only casualty since your family and friends will have been squeezed out of the scene long ago.

Extending the time available is not the answer. It's what you *do* during the time period that determines your effectiveness—and to a great extent, your health.

The Pareto Principle, named after an Italian economist-sociologist, Alfredo Pareto, states that the significant items in a given group normally constitute a relatively small portion of the total items in the group. The actual figures used are 20 percent and 80 percent. *So 20 percent of your activities accounts for 80 percent of the value of all your activities.*

The amazing thing about this "principle" is that it seems to hold true for everything. Twenty percent of the salesmen brings in 80 percent of the new business. Twenty percent of the items in inventory comprises 80 percent of the total value of the inventory. Twenty percent of your callers makes up 80 percent of your telephone time. Twenty percent of your employees causes 80 percent of your interruptions. Twenty percent of your paperwork provides 80 percent of your significant results. And so on.

The figures, 80 percent and 20 percent, may not be accurate, but the principle certainly holds true in practice. Believe it. *It will be the basis of your success in managing yourself with respect to time.*

Imagine a cube representing the time available for your work. If it represents a week's time, it would probably have a volume of about 35 hours. Filling this time cube are hundreds of activities. They fill the cube like a gas—important tasks, critical tasks, unnecessary tasks, unimportant tasks—all intermingled. No matter how few or how many activities you perform during a 35-hour time period, *they always fill the cube* (Parkinson's Law). If you are typical of the hundreds of executives I have talked to in time management seminars, there are many, many activities squeezed into your time cube all of which exert a considerable amount of pressure.

If you could separate those activities into categories you would find that about 20 percent are critical activities that account for about 80 percent of your results. The other 80 percent of your activities consists of important activities, unimportant but desirable activities, and unimportant and unnecessary activities.

Theoretically, you could then eliminate 80 percent of your activities and still maintain 80 percent of your results (Pareto's Principle).

I say *theoretically* because in all probability you could not maintain your job if you did. *You cannot sacrifice even 20 percent of your results.* You probably want *greater* results.

But you can: (1) eliminate the 5 or 10 percent of the activities which are unnecessary, and (2) delegate the desirable activities and some of the important activities. This would free up anywhere from 20 percent to 50 percent of your time.

You could then utilize this "spare time" by taking on more *critical* activities such as planning and innovating.

You must first determine the amount of time you want to spend on your job. Then you must eliminate or delegate the activities of lesser importance and fill the void with more important activities—activities that have bigger payoffs, accomplish significant results, and move you closer to your personal and business goals.

Take A Look At What You Do—And Why

How do you separate the activities into categories? How can you tell how important the activity really is? How do you decide which activities should be eliminated, delegated or retained?

Start by ruling off some sheets of paper similar to the one shown in exhibit 3. Then have a brainstorming session with yourself and list all the activities which you perform in the course of a year. Put everything down: making the coffee when you arrive early; sorting through invoices as a spot check on accounts receivable; touring the plant on a safety inspection each week; approving overtime slips; filing correspondence; making travel arrangements; chairing a monthly managers' meeting; and so on. Stay at it for a half hour or more and then leave it. Go about your work. Later, sit down, read the list and add to it. Leave it again. This time carry index cards or memo paper in your pocket and, whenever you are reminded of something else you do, jot it down. Transfer it to your sheet later. Do nothing else with these sheets for at least two weeks except to add items to the first column.

At the end of two weeks you should have quite a list —everything from ordering office supplies to conducting performance appraisals. In fact, I bet you'll be amazed at how full your time cube really is.

Do all of these activities really influence the profitability of the firm? Or the achievement of your personal and company goals? Well, let's find out.

COLUMN 1	COLUMN 2	COLUMN 3	COLUMN 4	COLUMN 5	COLUMN 6	COLUMN 7
What activities do I perform as part of my job and daily routine?	What is the reason I do them myself?	Can they be eliminated with no effect on my personal or company goals?	If the answer to column 3 is "no", can someone else do them?	If the answer to column 4 is "no", can someone else be trained to do them?	If the answer to column 5 is "no", can they be simplified, combined with other tasks or done better another way?	If the answer to columns 3, 4, 5 or 6 is "yes", when will I revisit action?

ACTIVITY – TIME ANALYSIS

© Harold L. Taylor Enterprises Ltd., 1990

Exhibit 3 Activity-Time Analysis

Next, review the items in column 1, and in column 2, write the *reason* you personally perform those tasks or activities. Be honest with yourself. After all, nobody else need ever see these worksheets. As an example, here are some of the reasons you might jot down:

"It's my job."

"No one else is qualified to do it."

"My boss assigned it to me."

"There's no one else to do it."

"The person who held this job before always did it."

"It's confidential. I *have* to do it."

"I *like* doing it. It's fun."

"It's in my job description."

"I do it better and faster than anyone else."

"It gives me a chance to show off my skill."

"I haven't got time to show someone else how to do it."

"I don't know why. I just ended up with the job."

"I let someone else do it once and it got loused up."

"It's personal. I wouldn't *want* anyone else to do it."

And so on.

Just the process of questioning why you do something might give you an idea as to how to eliminate it, simplify it or delegate it.

But let's look at some of those reasons you give for doing the job yourself. "It's my job" or "It's on my job description" or "My boss assigned it to me" are not very good reasons. Your job usually consists of a lot more responsibilities than you are able to handle by yourself. If you're a manager you're responsible for achieving certain results. The *way* you achieve them is left to your own ingenuity. Delegation is the sign of an effective manager. Changing methods, simplifying procedures or conserving valuable resources such as time and money through eliminating unnecessary jobs are all signs of an effective manager. And job descriptions are formed to *assist* employees, not to hamstring them. They can be changed if necessary. They're not carved in stone. Maybe you *do* have to perform these tasks personally. But the reason "It's on my job description" is usually not valid.

"No one else is qualified to do it" may be valid—if "qualified" means an employee has to be a ceramic engineer or physicist. But if it means *training* you can always schedule time for training.

"Everyone else is too busy to do it." How about yourself? Maybe other employees need to get organized, eliminate timewasters, and evaluate *their* jobs. You can probably help them to *unbusy* themselves.

"The person who held this job before always did it" is

on a par with "It's always been done this way." There may have been a legitimate reason for doing it at one time but situations change. Question it.

"I like doing it" should appear frequently if you enjoy your job. But it's not a legitimate reason for carrying on an activity that can be eliminated or delegated. There are probably a lot of enjoyable, rewarding, creative, *productive* activities you could become involved in if those enjoyable but *non-productive* jobs could be eliminated. And, if you enjoy certain tasks, just think how much your employees may enjoy them!

"There's no one else to do it" can only mean you have no employees reporting to you. And I certainly don't want to encourage upward delegation. But can you delegate it to outside resources, to your suppliers? Or better still, can you eliminate it or simplify it, or combine it with something else?

There are probably dozens of reasons why you do what you do. Question them all. Then move to column 3. Can they be eliminated? What would be the result if they were? Don't even consider delegating a task to someone else if it can be eliminated altogether. You would only be shifting your time problems to someone else. If you've listed most of your activities, and you really question their value, you will probably be able to eliminate a dozen or more without decreasing your effectiveness.

When you have eliminated everything you can, move to column 4. Can the tasks be delegated to someone else?

"Sure," you may say. "But they haven't got the time to do them." *Then make the time*. Help them eliminate, simplify or delegate some of their own tasks. Help them to get organized, utilize forms, shortcuts and checklists.

Help them to eliminate timewasters. Encourage them to manage *themselves* with respect to time.

Even if you have to hire an additional person (which is unlikely), it will still be more economical than getting yourself bogged down with too many essential but relatively unimportant activities. Compare the additional salary to the increased sales, reduced costs, and new opportunities that you could generate if you had the time. To fully earn your *own salary*, you must delegate almost everything except the critical and very important activities.

If the answer is still "no," move to column 5. Can someone be trained to do it within a reasonable length of time? It may take several weeks. Or perhaps an hour each day for several months. But is there someone currently on your staff who has the capacity to acquire the new skill? If "yes," launch a training schedule right away. Training is one of those *critical* activities which you probably haven't had time to do properly. Yet it's a big payoff activity, one that should replace some of those low-value activities you're getting rid of.

If the answer to column 5 is "no," it's probably a critical, high-value activity or one that is peculiar to the qualifications, technical skills or confidentiality of your position. Then you can only attempt to simplify it (column 6) and continue to do it.

It might seem strange not to have column 6 appear after column 3. It would seem normal to simplify an activity before delegating it. But I believe you should allow the delegatee to make the changes. In fact encourage it. Make suggestions if you must, but let your employees change the method to suit themselves. It's the end result you're interested in, not the method.

Principles Of Delegation

You now have plenty of jobs to delegate. But you also have time available to train and develop your people. You must set aside a block of time each week for this purpose. Place dates in column 7 after each task that you plan to eliminate, simplify or delegate. First, delegate those jobs that will free up the largest blocks of your time and then the routine, simple tasks that require little training time. You will be left with even more time available for delegating the others.

Delegation extends results from what you can *do* to what you can *control.* It frees time for more important tasks, allows you to plan more effectively, and helps relieve the pressure of too many jobs, too many deadlines, and too little time. Not only that, but it is one of the most effective ways of developing your subordinates.

Improper delegation, however, is worse than no delegation at all. It not only creates a greater demand on your own time, but messes up your employees' time as well. Be careful what you delegate, how you delegate, and to whom you delegate. Here are a few ground rules for effective delegation:

> *1. Don't delegate what you can eliminate.*
> If it's not important enough for you to do personally, it may not be important enough for your people to do either. Respect their time and their ability. Don't waste it on non-productive or unprofitable trivia. Your success can be multiplied a thousand times if you concentrate on the high-return jobs, and encourage your subordinates to do

likewise—don't spoil it by using your people as a dumping ground for "garbage" jobs.

2. *Delegate the things you don't want to delegate.*
We tend to hang on to the things we *like* doing even when they interfere with more important tasks, and even though our subordinates could probably do them just as well. Share the interesting work with your employees. One of the most important advantages of effective delegation is the fact that it enriches your subordinates' jobs. Don't limit your delegation to the boring, repetitive tasks—look for the interesting ones as well.

3. *Delegate, don't abdicate.*
Dumping jobs onto your subordinates and then disappearing is not delegation but organizational suicide. Delegation must be planned. Consult with your employees first; select people you think are both capable of doing the job and would like to do the job. Train them. Delegate gradually, insist on feedback, and then leave them alone.

4. *Delegate the objective, not the procedure.*
One of the bonuses you receive from effective delegation is the fact that in many cases the job is done better in the hands of someone else. Don't resent it; encourage it. Delegate the whole task for specific *results*, deemphasizing the actual *procedure*. Your subordinate, under less pressure, less harried, and with a fresh viewpoint, will likely improve upon the method you've been using. Review results, not the manner in which he or she arrived at them!

5. Don't always delegate to the most capable employees.

Delegation is one of the most effective methods of developing your people. Don't continually delegate to the most capable ones or they'll get stronger while the weak get weaker. Take the extra effort to spread delegation across the board, and develop a strong team with no weak links.

6. Trust your subordinates.

Be sure to delegate the authority as well as the responsibility. Don't continually look over their shoulders, interfere with their methods, or jump on them when they make mistakes. Be prepared to trade short-term errors for long-term results. Maintain control without stifling initiative.

Delegation is an absolute must if you are going to manage effectively and maintain control of your time. It's a critical activity and one that will increase your success.

CHAPTER 9

SLAY THE PAPERWORK DRAGON

Don't Play The Paperwork Game

Lee Grossman, in his book *Fat Paper: Diets for Trimming Paperwork*, claims that today the photocopier has replaced the water cooler as the center of office social life. He goes on to explain that in 1960, when the first plain paper copier was introduced, 3 billion copies were made. It has been estimated that 75 billion copies were made in 1973.

I shudder at the thought of how many copies are being made in 1981.

Grossman also related that according to Tab Products, a manufacturer of lateral filing systems, the average company:

—Wastes 65 cents out of every 81 spent for the record-making and filing operation
—Creates, types, and files hundreds of letters that should never be written
—Retains up to 70 percent more records than needed
—Never refers to 85 percent of their records, while 95

percent of all references are made to records under
three years old
—Uses 45 percent of filing-equipment space to store
duplicate copies and records of doubtful reference
value
—Facilitates creation of reports, 35 to 45 percent of
which are duplicates, overlapping or nonessential.

Imagine the cost of the office space housing the
millions of filing cabinets in this country.

In addition, companies rent hundreds of thousands of
cubic feet of outside space to house old records and
paperwork. At 10 to 15 cents a month per cubic foot,
that's a lot of money to store paper—most of which will
never be referred to again.

The cost of generating all this paperwork is also
increasing. According to Dartnell Institute, the cost of
the average business letter has increased 8.6 percent over
1979 to $6.07. In my opinion, this is an understatement.
When you consider the opportunities being sacrificed in
order to spend all that time generating paperwork, the
time cost would be phenomenal.

Paperwork is an expensive timewaster. What can you
do to decrease the amount of paperwork generated,
circulated and stored? Plenty.

*Don't write if you can accomplish the same thing by
'phone.* We write for a variety of reasons. Unfortunately
very few of them benefit the company. We write to save
our necks ("I *told* you that in my letter of August 21st.").
We write to become visible ("Send a copy of that to my
boss, his boss and her boss, oh yes, and to Alice, just in
case she *becomes* a boss."). We write to impress ("Let's
see now, what's a 26-letter word meaning 'bad'?"). We
write to justify our existence ("P.S. The volume of

paperwork alone justifies an additional staff person, however, through further increases in efficiency, we have succeeded in maintaining our staff at 12—plus 2 filing clerks."). We write for enjoyment ("I'm not a professional writer. Nor do I profess to be. I'm simple; but thorough. Limited in my vocabulary, but dedicated to my purpose. Demeaned but determined. Fraught but faithful, etc. etc.").

There *are* situations where putting it in writing is necessary—when people have to refer to it for reference, for instance. But too many people put it in writing for the wrong reasons, adding to the paperwork explosion unnecessarily. I recall reading in an American newsletter sometime ago about a manager who fought the "put it in writing" syndrome by saying he would not comply with written requests. When he received one he would return it with the comment, "Put it in a 'phone call."

Try writing less. When you receive a letter, resist the urge to grab a pen, and grab the 'phone instead. It's faster and cheaper. And you impress the sender with your prompt reply.

Throw out the letter afterwards. That is, in 80 percent of the cases throw it out. It's unlikely you'll ever have to refer to it again. Why clog up the files? The more you have filed, the longer it will take you to retrieve any of it if you *do* need it. Even if you threw out everything, you'd probably be safe. Remember, everybody else keeps *their* copies. Simply ask if they can send you a copy of the letter you misplaced. They'll love you for it. Not only will they feel they have a superior filing system, but you're helping justify its existence—along with their army of paper handlers.

I'm not serious about throwing out *everything*. But do keep your files as thin as possible. *Don't ever buy another filing* **cabinet**. Always thin out the ones you have instead. Make that clear to your employees as well. Encourage them to throw out something every afternoon before going home. Some people schedule at least one hour each week to sort through files, throwing out everything possible. A good idea.

It's unfortunate we don't have correspondence that self-destructs at a predetermined time because the older files get, the less useful they become. How often do you have to refer to a letter that was written two years ago? Or even two months ago? One way of speeding up the thinning out process is to determine *at the time of filing* how long you want the letter to remain in the files. So instead of writing "please file" on correspondence, write "Sept./82" with a brightly colored magic-marker. It takes no longer. And when sorting through files later, there's no necessity to read the letter before making a decision. If it's *after* Sept./82 it gets thrown out. If you have had to refer to that letter a few times, then you've also had a few opportunities to change your mind about its   importance—and to change the self-destruct date.

Using hanging files. Don't jam manila folders into a drawer or filing cabinet. A few seconds saved now will cost you precious minutes later. Manila folders combined with hanging files are ideal.

Don't let paperclips into your files. They foul up the works. Staple the reply letters to the originals.

Beware of double filing. I know of offices where three or more people keep copies of the same correspondence. What a terrible waste of time and money. So you (or your secretary) have to walk 50 feet to get something out of someone else's files. So what? How often does that happen? Compare that time with the time consumed in maintaining three filing systems. And the cost of the folders, cabinets and space.

Don't play the "paperwork game". Most time management experts claim that handling paper over and over again—putting it in piles on your desk, reshuffling, rehandling, rereading, is the biggest timewaster in the paperwork area. They urge you to keep it on the move. File it, scrap it, answer it—or circulate it for comments, opinions or additional information. But get it off your desk!

Well unfortunately, they've spawned a whole new breed of sophisticated paper shufflers. This hardy new strain of procrastinators devours other people's time as well as their own by playing what I call the "paperwork game." Whenever they have a piece of correspondence, a report or junk mail that they don't know what to do with, they send it to someone else with comments such as "For your information" or "What do you think?" or "Please comment." They have a half-hearted hope that the recipient might help with its disposition. They recognize a remote chance that the victim may even reply to the piece of correspondence or dispose of it in some other way. But the *real reason* they do it is to procrastinate under the guise of taking action. I call them "active procrastinators."

Here's how the game usually progresses. When the victims receive the paperwork, they procrastinate for a while themselves. This provides the instigator with temporary relief. Then they read the material (the first time consuming activity). Then they wonder why it was sent to them (the second time consuming activity). They usually spend quite a bit of time trying to determine its significance—what information they were expected to extract (this is particularly true when it is accompanied by a "For your information" notation). The amount of time they spend on this activity varies directly with the sender's position in the company. For example, a president can waste hours of an employee's time with a stroke of the pen.

Finally, the victim returns it to its rightful owner usually with some vague scribble such as "noted" or "definitely" or "looks okay to me."

The "active procrastinator" has accomplished nothing except waste other people's time as well as his own. Everything he sends out eventually comes home to roost.

There's nothing wrong with asking for information or requesting comments before replying to an *important memo*. Even then, you should explain what information you need and when you need it. But don't ever allow yourself to play the "paperwork game" and circulate unimportant correspondence, literature or junk mail. Respect your employees' and associates' time.

When you *do* circulate important literature or correspondence, indicate its final destination. If you want it to end up in the wastebasket, say so. Otherwise the recipient may waste time deciding what to do with it. And chances are it'll end up back on your desk. Or worse still, in the filing system.

In the United States alone enough documents and paper are filed each year to fill 65 million filing cabinets and keep over 2½ million file clerks busy. If that doesn't frighten you, nothing will.

Don't Waste Time On Words

Be stingy with the time you spend on correspondence. Get someone to screen your mail if possible. Have your secretary or assistant reply to routine letters. Ignore trivial requests. Don't send acknowledgment letters if you don't have to. Reply to simple requests by writing directly on the letter and returning it. Use a rubber stamp or label with the following explanation:

SPEED REPLY

In order to give the fastest possible response, we have made these marginal notes. In this instance we believe you prefer speed to formality. We have made a copy for our files.

Hopefully you *won't* make a copy for your files. But it makes the sender feel better if you say you do.

If you feel the person is too important to be subjected to the above shortcuts—and you can't accomplish your purpose with a 'phone call—then by all means, write. But not longhand. Use a cassette recorder. Dictation is over twice as fast as writing longhand. You may feel uncomfortable at first but with practice you will be able to dictate clear, concise letters.

Be sure to let your secretary know when you want the letters typed. Put deadlines on everything. Make only those copies that are absolutely necessary. Don't waste other people's time as well as add to the paperwork overload. Don't proofread your letters. Let your secretary do that. Don't even sign them all. Don't even *write* them all. Let your secretary develop some writing skills. Use form letters for high-volume, routine correspondence.

If you initiate a letter, don't be held up waiting for a reply. Use the "Unless I hear from you . . ." approach.

If you *need* feedback, put a copy in your follow-up file. Don't type another letter if the first one isn't answered. Photostat it and stamp it with the following message:

REMINDER

Your reply to the attached letter has not yet been received. Please re-read this photocopy and let us hear from you.

Incidentally, rubber stamps are great timesavers. And they're inexpensive. If you find you're writing the same notations over and over again, put them on stamps.

Address your letters to only one person if you want a quick response. If you address it to two people they'll probably wait for each other to reply. Cover only one topic per memo. If you must cover several topics, list them separately and number them. Make it easy for the reader to reply. You don't want to be kept waiting. Try a rubber stamp on *your* letters:

Reply here to save time.
Photostat for your records.

Fold your letters with the masthead out so the reader can spot your message quickly. And if you want a particular message to stand out put it in the first sentence, underline it, or add it as a *P.S.* It's been proven that the parts of a letter that are read first are the opening sentence and the postscript. That is, if the letter is short enough to be typed on one page.

And that's your next challenge—to be informal, courteous and brief when writing. Don't stuff your sentences with big words, unnecessary adjectives, and ambiguous phrases. Don't waste time searching for the "right" words—letters tend to become wordy, formal and frequently unintelligible. Remember that the objective of a letter is to communicate, not to impress.

If you must write letters, try to retain your own personality. Be simple. Informal. Natural. And come to the point quickly.

Don't get hung up on grammar or vocabulary. The trend is towards informality and no one will ridicule you for starting a sentence with "and" or leaving out the odd verb or even for allowing a participle or two to dangle. It's more important to have your letters carry that personal touch. To have them capture the reader's attention. And to write with the reader's wants and needs in mind.

This doesn't mean you should use poor grammar intentionally.

Standard English gives a greater assurance that you and your reader will be on the same wavelength. But acceptable business style is literate, not literary. Ostentation or pomposity *does not* impress. It only arouses suspicion in the mind of the reader.

Here are a few suggestions to keep your letters short, natural, *and* more effective:

1. Keep your sentences short.
It's okay to have a long one now and then. In fact it breaks the monotony. But keep them separated with lots of short, simple sentences.

2. Use familiar, simple words.

Instead of searching for long words, designed to impress, try looking for short ones or two-syllable words to substitute for the long ones. And stay away from jargon.

3. Use verbs in the active voice.

Don't say "It was decided at a meeting of the board of directors . . ." Try instead, "The board of directors decided . . ." Using the active voice makes your letters come alive. And cuts down the word count.

4. Avoid tiresome expressions.

Be original. Stay away from expressions like "a few well-chosen words," "assuring you of our prompt attention," or "attached please find." Most expressions of this type can be eliminated altogether.

5. Be direct.

Don't use two or three words when one will do: "at your earliest convenience" is "soon"; "due to the fact that" is "because."

6. Use adjectives sparingly.

And stay clear of those senseless, unnecessary adjectives that add nothing to the meaning: for example, "*practical* experience" (is there any other kind?) and "establish *necessary* criteria" (would anyone want to establish *unnecessary* criteria?)

7. Write in the first person.

You wouldn't talk on the 'phone that way, so why write that way? "I hear" is a lot more natural and more simple than "It was brought to my attention." And it requires fewer words.

It's oversimplifying things to say "write like you talk." When we talk we usually keep repeating ourselves and that just isn't necessary when writing.

To become an effective writer you have to work at it. Keep asking yourself if that adjective is necessary, or whether there's a shorter way of saying something.

With practice you will be able to write effectively using only half as many words. And that saves time for you *and* the reader.

8. Keep business reports business-like.

Keep your reports short. Your solution to the problem, and your recommendations, are what people want—not your play by play description of everything that happened. Business reports should not read like suspense novels. Be direct. Keep them simple. Be brief. Sure, you put a lot of time and effort into your investigation, but why take it out on the reader? Summarize the conclusions and recommendations on the first page. Let them read about your reasoning and all your work later, if they have time. And tack all those detailed statistics, charts and graphs on the end as an addendum. Always keep in mind that you're being paid for results, not words.

CHAPTER 10

DON'T FALL INTO
THE MEETING TRAP

Conduct Effective Meetings

"Oh, there you are Sam." You glance at your watch for the third time in as many minutes. "For a minute we thought you weren't coming." Sam apologizes in the form of a play by play description of the traffic along a five-mile stretch of highway 401. After listening a respectable, but unnecessary, length of time you again take charge as chairman. "Well, John's the only one not here yet. And we *are* 20 minutes late already. What say we start the meeting and we can fill in John when he arrives? According to Sam here, he may be stuck in traffic for quite a while." Sam nods enthusiastically and relates two and a half more minutes of traffic tales which had slipped his mind when he first arrived.

The meeting gets underway and by the time John arrives you have heard seven warm-up jokes, witnessed three treks to the coffee pot, and a good round of discussion on the first agenda item. After hearing the latest traffic report and an enlightening lecture on carburetor icing you invite John to grab a coffee while you

quickly "bring him up to date." Two more jokes and a
flippant remark from Bill Watson, the director of engineering, slip out before you get the meeting under
control again. The flippant remark went something like
this: "I just figured out that based on an estimated
average hourly salary of $24 per hour, with 14 of us, this
meeting has already cost us $360, and we've hardly got
started." The remark inspired a lot of laughter.

But it was no laughing matter.

The business meeting is one of the most maligned
management activities in existence. It has been accused
of being a time wasting, work disrupting, fruitless
exercise in idleness. And improperly handled it can
become just that.

But meetings *can* be effective management tools.
Conducted properly they can be used to gain cooperation
and promote team spirit, share information, solve problems and eliminate the time consuming repetition of
individual contacts. They can be used to generate ideas,
squelch rumors, assign responsibilities, gain consensus
and initiate action. They can strengthen close working
relationships, improve morale, motivate employees and
improve communications.

But before calling a meeting, make sure that one is
really necessary. If a telephone call, a memo or conference call will accomplish the same purpose, use it.
Meetings are costly. Assuming you spend only four
hours each week in meetings, over a 10-year period you
will have spent the equivalent of a full year sitting in
meetings. Multiply that by your annual salary and do
likewise for all the other participants, and you have a
sizeable cost. And that doesn't take into consideration
the opportunities lost by not working on profit-
generating tasks during that one year equivalent. Ac-

cording to Doyle and Strauss in their book, *How Meetings Work,* there are over 11 million meetings held every day in the United States alone. Don't add to that costly total unless absolutely necessary.

Schedule your meetings late in the day if you want it to be a short one. Business has a tendency to move quickly as it approaches five o'clock. But if you need all day and it's worth the time and expense, schedule the whole day.

Successful meetings, like anything else, must be planned. And planning involves advance preparation, timing, attendance, agenda—and most important, a statement of objectives to be accomplished.

Respect the time of others—invite only those who can contribute to or gain from the meeting. Be prepared to excuse people early when they can no longer gain from or contribute to the remaining topics.

Set objectives in such a way that you can measure the results at a later date. Do you want people to understand certain procedures, increase sales, reduce costs, or solve a problem? Include the objectives both on the agenda and on a flipchart or blackboard in the meeting room.

Develop a detailed outline or agenda and send it out to all participants well in advance. Detail the starting time, ending time, time allocated to each topic area and the individuals responsible for reports or presentations. Make sure this vital information stands out. Make it clear that any written reports should be distributed well in advance of the meeting so the participants can review them without spending valuable meeting time. When drawing up the agenda, make sure the most important items appear first. Poll the participants in advance. Make sure you know what they want discussed and what they have to report. And tell them what you expect of *them.*

They should be prepared and aware of the time allocated for their presentation or report. Above all, they should understand the *objectives* of the meeting. Don't cram too much into the agenda. Skipping quickly over critical issues in order to finish on time is *not* a timesaver.

Select the meeting place carefully. It should take place away from the normal work area and needless interruptions. The room should be well ventilated, not too warm, and with enough space to allow the participants to stretch out. The room doesn't have to be luxurious. In fact, a study conducted in 1973 by R. M. Greene & Associates indicated a direct correlation between room beauty and meeting efficiency—*the more beautiful, the less efficient.* Use visual aids of some kind—flipchart, blackboard, or overhead projector—to increase attention.

Start the meeting on time, regardless. If you're the only one there on time, talk to yourself until the others arrive! Don't recap with every late arrival. Delaying the meeting simply encourages lateness. At the start, explain what will be covered and why. Restate the objectives. Keep to the agenda and don't allow participants to take off on tangents.

If someone starts a conversation about something trivial cut him or her off politely with a remark such as "I know that problem's in good hands with you, Jack. We won't discuss it here." You might reduce petty arguments if you seat adversaries on the same side of the table, but apart from one another. If they can't see each other they won't lock horns as often. Remember, if your meeting starts to drift in a direction that will not help to reach your objective, pull it back on course. And fast. But don't get hung up on parliamentary procedure unless you're a member of parliament. The name of the game is to get results.

Guard against one or two people monopolizing the discussion, and encourage everyone to participate and watch for those non-verbal signals that indicate someone doesn't understand, objects, or wishes to speak. Listen more than you talk. One study revealed that the average leader took 60 percent of the conference time. If it's one-way communication you want, forget about a meeting and send a memo instead.

The meeting is over when you have accomplished your objectives, so don't let it drag on. Summarize the actions to be taken and make sure responsibilities are clear. Issue minutes promptly, with actions clearly highlighted. Ideally, a form should replace normal minutes to highlight the decisions reached, the action required, the person responsible for follow-up and the date the action is to be completed. But if you need formal minutes, use this short version as a cover form. Don't force people to dig through pages and pages of minutes searching for items they are supposed to look after. Chances are, they won't. And nonaction is a great and costly timewaster.

Always evaluate your meetings afterwards. Ask what could be improved next time. If your magic-markers ran dry or the overhead transparency bulb burned out and you had no spare, it should never happen the second time. *Planning for any meeting starts with the end of the last meeting.* Inadequate planning steals precious time. For example, if you have ten people in attendance, earning an average of $20 per hour, the meeting is costing you *$3.34 per minute*. If you only lose 15 minutes looking for a spare bulb or magic-marker, this simple slip in planning has cost you $50.10.

In the same way, you can see that a 4-hour meeting will cost you $801.60. And that's an understatement because time spent in meetings is time taken away from other critical activities. Judge the importance of a meeting by the results you get from it.

'Cause it's costing you!

Be An Active Participant

You must conduct meetings effectively in order to use up less time. But I'll bet you spend more time in other people's meetings than you do in your own. How do you control *those?*

Well you can't control the meeting completely, but *you can control yourself with respect to the meetings.* Don't attend time wasting meetings. If you have doubts about the necessity of your presence, ask. Maybe you were on the invitation list so you wouldn't feel you were being passed over. There's a lot of politics at play in organizations. Some people go to great lengths to observe protocol. After all, they wouldn't want you to get your nose out of joint. "Jack, this meeting next Thursday. Is it really imperative that I be there?" That's all it takes. You may be surprised at the reply. If the person hesitates, go on to explain the critical tasks you're working on. If it's your boss, he or she is as concerned as you about how you spend your time. Maybe a copy of the minutes and a brief 'phone call to the chairman afterwards is all that is necessary to keep you onstream with the meeting's objectives. But don't attend unless you have to—unless you feel that particular meeting is a high priority, critical activity.

If the only reason you have to be there is to present a report, ask if you can attend only *that* portion of the meeting. There should be an agenda detailing the time allotted for your report. If there isn't, ask for one. And make sure you know the objective of the meeting. If there's no objective it's not worth attending and you'll be doing yourself and your company a favor by feigning illness.

People should not be subjected to four or five-hour meetings if only a half hour is of importance to them and if they cannot increase the other attendees' effectiveness by being present. So don't hesitate to suggest that you leave early to fulfill other commitments. And don't forget the alternative of sending someone else in your place.

If you have considered the above alternatives, and decide to attend the full meeting yourself, then it's probably because you feel it's important enough to warrant your attendance—and your time. But be on guard. Meetings can have meaningful objectives and timed agendas, and still take twice as long as they should. It depends on the chairman and the other participants. And on yourself.

Before you attend a meeting, be prepared. Have all your meeting material in one folder or binder. If it's an on-going committee, you should have a binder with material separated by tabbed dividers. Break down the categories as much as possible so you can find material quickly. Minutes of previous meetings should have all important items highlighted with a yellow marker. Invariably time is wasted by people searching for past records, reports or documents. If your binder is complete and properly organized, you can save everyone some time.

If you have to submit a report, complete it early and distribute it in advance. But bring spare copies with you. There are always people who claim they never received it. (There are even a few who admit they never looked at it or forgot to bring it.) Bring plenty of pens, pencils and paper. Also a 3-hole punch, stapler, and calculator.

Always bring some routine work with you. In the event the meeting does turn into a timewaster and you are helpless to keep in control or leave without being fired, at least you will be able to get some productive work done. It must be routine, since meetings are not conducive to concentration. Don't bring magazines. Reading at a meeting is an insult regardless of the incompetence of the chairman. At least you will be less obvious if you are doing written work. It may even look like you're taking notes.

Arrive on time but never be early. Early arrivals usually get involved in non-productive conversations. Work on your routine tasks until the meeting starts, which means you normally need quite a lot of routine work. Choose your seat carefully. If you don't smoke, stay clear of those areas the ashtrays have gravitated to. Avoid sitting next to the notorious joke tellers, loud talkers, or the attendees who fan all their materials in front of them to cover all the table space. Don't sit near the coffee pot, telephone or doorway or you'll be constantly interrupted. Pick a roomy spot between two introverts so you can concentrate on the meeting's objectives and help speed it along its way.

During the meeting, help keep the chairman on track. If someone starts discussing an entirely different issue, quickly ask the chairman if this is to be added to the agenda. And don't be sidetracked yourself. If the joke-ster asks, "Have you heard the one about . . ." quickly reply, goodnaturedly, "Yes, it's hilarious. Mr. Chairman, on that last point, have we concluded that . . ." Don't react emotionally to anything being discussed. Don't allow yourself to be baited. It's a business meeting so keep it impersonal. Anger, resentment, and petty grievances not only waste time but make you less effective at making rational decisions.

Don't pass notes to the chairman or others. Communication stops while notes are being passed because everybody's mind is on that note. It interrupts the meeting, creates a feeling of resentment among some participants, and *wastes time*. If you have something to say, speak up.

And don't feel you *have* to talk. Speak only if you have something to say that will help reach the meeting's objectives.

Be an active listener and make notes, recording major points, decisions reached and follow-ups required. If you have found it necessary to attend the meeting, then it's necessary to get all you can out of it. You want value for your money. And you're not at the mercy of the chairman. You owe it to yourself and the others to keep the meeting productive. For example, if you see that it's approaching lunch hour and there's only about an hour of business left to be conducted, suggest that lunch be delayed until the meeting is finished. Don't waste time on another meeting "start-up" unless absolutely necessary.

When it's all over, don't wait for the minutes to arrive. You may wait a long time. And you may forget what certain statements in the minutes referred to. Instead, take action right away based on the information in your Meeting Participant's Action Sheet. You've got the "do it now" habit.

So do it.

Instead, take action right away based on the information in your Meeting Participant's Action Sheet. You've got the "do it now" habit.

So do it.

CHAPTER 11

MAKE THE MOST
OF BUSINESS TRIPS

Manage Your Travel Time

Many businessmen and businesswomen are now travelling to such an extent that effective utilization of travel time becomes a major factor in success. Here are some suggestions on how to manage your travel time more effectively.

Use a travel agent. Don't waste your time or your secretary's time by encountering busy signals or being placed on hold. Or trying to decipher the dozens of possible flight connections. A good travel agent can get you to your destination with a minimum of plane changes, stops, and airport delays.

But don't forget to tell the agent what you expect. Specify direct flights where possible, connections involving the minimum delay and avoiding the busier airports. Where possible, avoid arrivals and departures that coincide with local traffic rush hours. Have your tickets well in advance. And don't forget contingency flights in case you miss connections. Consider flying first class. It assures you of a good seat, plenty of room for work and relaxation, minimum delay in boarding and leaving the airplane and less chance of noisy children and other distractions.

If you travel economy class, arrive at the airport early for good seat selection. Remember, aisle seats have more space for carry-on luggage. Extra leg space is available in the front row of seats and at the emergency exits. Avoid the washroom area—it will get crowded on longer flights.

Always phone the destination hotel to reconfirm your room. And check the airline to find out if the flight is delayed. Make any arrangements for car rentals in advance. Use the ones at the airports for convenience.

Photostat your itinerary and leave copies with your secretary and spouse. Include such things as the address and 'phone number of the hotel. While you're at it, photostat your credit cards just in case they get lost or stolen. It's faster than copying down all the numbers.

When packing, conserve space. Where possible, limit your luggage to a carry-on bag to avoid waiting at luggage turntables. If you travel frequently, keep a "personal effects" kit always packed, ready to go. It should contain all those essential items such as toothpaste, toothbrush, shampoo, hairbrush—the dozens of items most frequently forgotten. Replenish after every trip.

Overpacking is a timewaster. Take only half of what you think you'll need. For short trips stick to one basic color for clothes. That way you can get away with only one pair of shoes and other accessories.

Have standard checklists for warm weather and cold weather destinations so you won't forget anything. Make one as you pack for your next 2 or 3-day trip. Make duplicate copies for future use. And don't leave the job of packing until the last minute.

If you must use a large suitcase, make sure it's tough and sturdy with a combination lock. Have an identification tag inside as well in case the one on the outside gets torn off. For security reasons, don't use your home address. Identify the bags with business card addresses. Put a splash of color or bright label on the suitcase so it can be spotted easily on the luggage turntable or conveyer belt.

Consider taking a taxi or airport limousine to the airport. You can relax, read, or prepare notes en route. And you conserve time and energy by not having to find a parking space and make the long trek with a briefcase and luggage to the proper departure area. Reserve the taxi a day in advance.

Bring along plenty of reading material and paperwork for those unavoidable waits and delays. Work on priority material early in the flight while you're at your peak. Leave reading material and routine paperwork for times when you're feeling sluggish. Always relax just before touchdown. And don't fight the crowds when deplaning from economy class. Relax. If you have luggage to retrieve you'll be waiting later anyway.

If you don't need a car at your destination, don't rent one. Save time and effort by taking taxis. Avoid the airport buses. They're usually late, uncomfortable and not conducive to either reading or resting. If your meeting or other business can be scheduled at the airport hotel, better still.

When at your hotel, review your itinerary and utilize your time wisely. You have some excellent uninterrupted time at your disposal. Consider having your breakfast in your hotel room (order it the night before).

Use the time you save for preparing for the day's activities. It's also more relaxing than fighting the coffee-shop crowds.

By planning your business trips in advance, spending a little extra money, and taking advantage of the free time at your disposal, frequent trips no longer become a major timewaster.

And If You Drive

If a manager works 8 hours per day, and drives 10,000 miles in a year at 40 mph, he or she spends over 31 days travelling. If you have 100 employees travelling the same 10,000 miles, you are paying the equivalent of another employee just to cover the cost of travel time.

Unfortunately, we can't simply beam ourselves to our destination in Star Trek fashion. But what we can do is to more effectively utilize our own travel time and encourage our employees to do likewise.

Once the route has been designed to minimize travelling time, there are still several ways of productively utilizing the time still spent behind the wheel.

Professional development:
There are excellent cassette tapes available, everything from condensations of bestselling books to motivational and sales training tapes. This is far more productive than listening to the same news over and over again on the radio. And it can reap benefits in terms of professional development.

Dictation:
Letters, reports, sales quotes, follow-up lists, and ideas can all be dictated into a small pocket recorder while driving. This will reduce the time normally spent on

paperwork later. It also prevents you from forgetting those creative ideas that seem to pop up out of nowhere.

Planning:

Driving time can be utilized for planning the day, rehearsing a sales presentation, solving a problem or reviewing and evaluating the day's activities. To be effective, however, you must be able to discipline yourself. Your mind has a tendency to wander and engage in a little extracurricular daydreaming.

Relaxation:

You mustn't lose sight of the fact that on occasion you should do nothing except relax and listen to music. It clears the cobwebs after a particularly hectic morning. A relaxation break is productive when it revitalizes you for the tasks ahead.

Quiet hour:

During a heavy traffic tie-up or when a long drive has made you particularly weary, you should consider pulling off the road and setting up office for an hour. In fact it might be a good idea to make it a habit every day —perhaps while you're still in a client's parking lot. Your briefcase should be equipped with everything you need to schedule your next day's clients, summarize reports and statistics, and update your log book. This quiet hour in the car assures you of interruption-free time away from the hustle and bustle of the office. Unencumbered with telephone interruptions and visitors, your paperwork can be dispensed with quickly.

Here are a few more hints on saving time while on the road:

1. Plan your travel route in advance. Make sure your latest calls are closest to your home or office. You will waste less time sitting in rush hour traffic.
2. Use a checklist to ensure that you have everything you

need for the trip, including change for pay telephones, addresses and phone numbers, and a spare ignition key. Think the trip through chronologically as you make the list so you won't forget anything.

3. Be sure to take reading material with you for those inevitable waits in reception rooms.

4. Keep a record of all your calls. List what went right, what went wrong, follow-ups required, problems to be solved. And do it immediately following the call. Don't leave it until you get back to the office. Relying on your memory can be a major timewaster.

5. If you have to travel a considerable distance to make one call, determine what other prospects you can visit while in the area. You'll reduce the travel time per call.

A McGraw-Hill survey reveals that the average salesperson only spends 39 percent of his or her time in front of prospects, while travelling and waiting time take up 32 percent. If you're a salesperson just think what the results would be if face to face selling time could be increased to 50 percent.

This could be easily accomplished if travel and waiting time were utilized to dictate letters and reports, dispense with paperwork, plan, summarize sales calls, listen to tapes, and anything else that normally fills the 29 percent of a salesperson's job still remaining.

Whether you travel by plane, train, bus or car, you will encounter delays and periods of non-productive time. Your effectiveness depends on how you use it. And you will use it to advantage if you are prepared.

Equip your briefcase with standard items you are likely to need. Make it your office away from the office. In the large pockets stow away road maps, envelopes, stationery, scratch pad, promotional material, and reading material. In the smaller pockets keep a pocket calculator, pens, business cards, and cheques.

Make up a travel "junk" box containing everything you've ever found you needed while on a trip: dimes for pay telephones; quarters for tolls; postage stamps for that card or letter; highlighter for reading material; staples; pins; and thread.

The more organized you become, the less effort it takes to become even more organized. And the more time you'll have for those important things in your life.

CHAPTER 12

DON'T LET OTHERS
STEAL YOUR TIME

Timesaving Hang-Ups

"Yes, Ralph . . . right . . . uh huh . . ." You squirm in your chair impatiently. "Right . . . well, I'll get back to you as soon as I get word. . . ." Egad! does this man ever stop talking? You move the receiver away from your ear and stare at it. You can still hear the voice clearly. Monotonous. Redundant. Incessant. You join the conversation again in an attempt to end it. "Okay, Ralph. But I have to go now. Someone is waiting for me in the lobby." You lie in desperation. The voice continues, oblivious to your agony. "Oh, oh, there goes the other phone. Ralph, I'm going to have to . . . yes . . ." He's unreal! He just won't shut up. You glance at your watch for the tenth time. The one-sided conversation has been going on for over twenty minutes! "Right . . . Okay, I'll . . ." Suddenly you get an idea; you read it somewhere in a time management book. You fight your way back into the conversation. Your voice takes on a new vibrance. You're obviously interested in carrying on this conversation. "Well, Ralph, I can see why you're concerned . . ." Your hand moves to the little button on the 'phone. "In fact I'm grateful that you called. Why only the other . . ." Then suddenly, in the middle of your sentence, your finger slaps down the button cutting off the conversation. You have just hung up on yourself.

But Ralph won't know that. Nobody hangs up on *himself*. Ralph will think it's the fault of the switchboard or the telephone company. He'll be frantically dialing again right now. You dash to the switchboard. "Alice," you gasp. "If anyone calls I'm on the other line." Alice is beautiful. She nods and smiles knowingly.

"You mean only if it's Ralph?" she asks.

"Yes." You sigh. The relaxed, peaceful sigh of the reprieved. "Only if it's Ralph."

Chances are, the above scene will never occur. You don't know anyone as talkative as Ralph. Or do you? Even if you do, hanging up is a last resort. But make up your mind right now that people will not waste your time. You will not allow it. You did not organize yourself, your office, files, and methods just to conserve precious time for others to steal.

When driving a car you have to drive defensively. You have to guard against other people causing an accident. It's the same with your time and life. You have to guard against other people causing a time wastage. Time which is valuable, which belongs to you.

The telephone is the timewaster's most common weapon. So tread cautiously.

The way you use the telephone at home should be different from the way you use it at work. Its prime purpose at work is not for *socializing*. Be polite, but be brief. Ask a person how he or she is, and you may get a twenty minute discourse on the pros and cons of a hemorrhoidectomy. When Jack calls, answer cheerfully, "Hi, Jack, what can I do for you?" It's not impolite, but it gets the caller to the point of the call a lot faster.

Control the conversation. In meetings, a chairperson controls the conversation and keeps it on course. Appoint yourself chairperson and direct the conversation to the objective of the call. Ask as few questions as possible. It will keep the conversation short. Like a meeting, once the objective is reached, the call is over. End it politely, but promptly. Don't be afraid to say "Goodbye."

When someone asks for an appointment to see you, find out what he or she wants. Chances are you'll be able to settle it right there on the 'phone. But if you have already agreed to meet with the caller, don't waste time discussing it on the 'phone as well.

The telephone is there for *your* convenience, not the reverse. You're not expected to be at its beckoning call. Have calls screened during certain "quiet hours" when you want to work on priority tasks. If you have no one to screen your calls, get an answering service. You can't be effective while constantly reaching for the 'phone—unless fielding telephone calls *is* your job. If you want the telephone to work for you, and not against you, you're going to have to observe certain time saving strategies:

1. Group the call-backs. Get in the habit of accumulating your messages and returning the calls in a group. Just before noon is a good time, since conversations tend to be briefer when they threaten to interfere with lunch. About 4:30 P.M. is a good time to return the afternoon calls.

2. Dial your own numbers. It takes just as much of your time to get the secretary to place your calls as it does to make them yourself. With touchtone telephones, direct dialing, 'phone rests, and routine "filler" work, even busy signals won't result in much lost time. So why waste your secretary's time? His or her salary comes out of the same pocket.

3. Record the best time of the day or week to get through to the people you 'phone on a regular basis (based on experience). Include this information in your telephone directory.

4. Install touchtone telephones. It takes at least four times as long to dial using the conventional 'phones.

5. Don't get in the habit of holding unless you have a lot of routine work you can do while you wait. Leave a message instead.

6. Before making a call, quickly jot down the points you want to discuss so you won't forget anything.

7. If the person you're calling is not there, try to get the information you need from someone else rather than leave a message to call back.

8. Have your assistant screen incoming calls and handle as many as possible.

9. When your staff takes messages, make sure they record what the call is about and the telephone number so you won't have to look it up.

10. Arrange your call-backs in order of importance in case you're interrupted before you finish.

11. Always have routine jobs available (signing

letters, filing, etc.) to fill waiting time when making a series of calls.

12. If some callers are long winded, try letting them talk themselves out. Silence tends to end a conversation sooner.

13. If you have a gossip on the other end of the line, excuse yourself by being "wanted on the other line."

14. If you need information to allow you to work on your priority items, make those calls early in the morning to get on that person's "to do" list for the day.

15. Make notes on all calls. They're just as important as meetings. Use the "Telephone & Visitors Log" suggested in Chapter 5.

A telephone does not have to be a timewaster. It can be a real timesaver. It can save writing time. Many letters you receive are simply asking a question or requesting some information. Resist the urge to write back. Pick up the 'phone and give your answer verbally. It's usually faster, less expensive, and impresses the sender.

The telephone can also save meeting time. Conference calls not only save the time of the participants but also eliminate any travel costs. But *you* must be in control. Don't let others use the telephone as an offensive weapon.

It can be very offensive.

Discourage Drop-Ins

Even though you're able to control those telephone callers you will still have to guard against those individuals who interrupt you in person. They could be from outside the company or they could be your boss, peers or employees.

A closed door during your quiet hour will lend you some protection. But you can't have your door closed all day.

The first thing you should do is make certain your assistant, secretary or receptionist realizes that you don't see drop-in visitors without an appointment. At least you shouldn't—except in rare cases—or you will soon lose control of your own time. Always be "busy" to unannounced callers and they'll soon get the message. On those rare cases when you want to talk to the unexpected visitors, do it in the reception area or lobby. Don't let them into your office. If they manage to barge in, stand up immediately and terminate the conversation while standing. Don't invite them to sit down and don't offer to take their coats or give them coffee. It may sound terribly impolite, but they don't deserve, nor should they expect, much of an audience if they drop in unannounced.

When someone calls for an appointment, try to settle the matter right there on the 'phone. In most cases a meeting isn't necessary.

If you must meet, make sure you find out how much time the visitor expects it will take. People usually underestimate the time intentionally in order to get your agreement. If they say "only about ten minutes," tell them you'll schedule fifteen "just in case." Then make sure you schedule another appointment—or an imaginary one—right after it. Don't allow open-ended visits.

If their time is up and they're reluctant to leave, use conversation terminators such as "Fine, I'll get right on it" or "Well, it was great talking to you." Turn on the old body language. Glance at your watch, close the folder, stand up. Let the visitor know the discussion is over. If you feel it's important to continue, fine. But first call your secretary on the intercom to confirm that it's time for your next appointment. Then have it delayed 5 minutes. Both real and imaginary appointments can usually be delayed with equal ease.

Don't hesitate to come right out and tell the visitor that you have another appointment. It's your time. Control it.

Your employees can sometimes be the worst offenders. Don't let them "pop in" every ten minutes. Tell them to "save up" all but urgent problems before making a trip to your office. Even urgent problems will usually be communicated faster by telephone or intercom. And don't forget to insist on suggested *solutions* to those problems. Effective delegation will greatly reduce the need for interruptions by employees.

It's more difficult to control interruptions by the boss. But a good boss will respect employees' time. If you have a choice, meet the boss in his or her office. That way you can leave as soon as the objective of the visit is reached. It's a good idea to have some priority task—that is important to the boss—on the go. It's a great reason for breaking away from a non-productive conversation.

In spite of your efforts, interruptions will still occur. Accept it. It's part of a manager's job. But allow for those interruptions when you schedule your tasks.

Make Crises A Learning Experience

Crises occur frequently. But they shouldn't *recur* frequently. Not the same crises. As soon as they happen, take action to see that they don't happen again.

Planning can't prevent a crisis from happening in the first place because you can't foresee it happening, but planning must start the moment it *does* happen. You must plan to prevent the same consequences from happening again should an item be suddenly out of stock, or a machine breaks down, or a key employee quits. As a result you lose production. Then is the time to plan so the same incident doesn't recur. Or if it does, plan so production isn't affected the same way.

Crises will always occur. And handling them is part of your job as a manager. But don't let the same crises repeat themselves again and again. It's poor management. It's costly. And it's time consuming.

Know Your Job; But "No" Everyone Else's

Don't be trapped into doing everyone else's work for them. Cooperation is fine; but not if it's always paid for with *your* time. There always seems to be one member of the office staff, one member of a family, one member of a club, who constantly gets stuck with the "joe" jobs. And it's nobody's fault but their own.

There's only one way to say "no"—and that is quickly, briefly, and forcefully. You don't owe anyone long explanations about why you can't do something. Give an explanation and you leave the door open. If you tell Sally you can't accept the job of social convenor for the local parent's association because you're too busy with other clubs' evening activities, she'll come back with a program committee's job for you "that only takes a few lunch hours each month." Just say "Sorry, I can't," and leave it at that.

It's your time. It's your life. And it's your right to say "no" to any volunteer jobs, errands or other activities that do not fall within your sphere of responsibility. Not that you should always say "no," but chances are you should be saying it more often.

Try a little experiment with your own employees. When they ask, "Can you help me with this?" simply say "No." A look of disbelief, perhaps shock, will greet you. They'll stare at you for what seems the longest time. Lost for words. They just can't cope with an answer of "no." Nobody simply says "no" to anyone.

Of course you wouldn't handle your employees that way. But you wouldn't get involved in *their* problems either. You would ask what the trouble was, what they suggest as a solution, offer a supportive comment or two and send them on their way. Don't allow upward delegation. Your desk is no place for half-finished reports, memos or other paperwork that belong to your subordinates. When they ask for solutions or answers, seek *their* recommendations. Comment. Give advice. But don't ever take on a task that they are responsible for.

Some employees use the boss as a way of procrastinating. They hand in *outlines* of reports, *drafts* of letters, *ideas* on projects with the excuse that they want you to review or evaluate their approach before they proceed. *You* become the bottleneck. They can't proceed until you've had time to review what they've done to date.

And knowing how busy you are they feel they're buying a lot of time. Don't let it happen. Accept only completed projects.

Know your job. And "no" their's.

CHAPTER 13

HELP EMPLOYEES MANAGE THEIR TIME

Time Wastage By Employees

Time is an expensive commodity. For example, if 20 employees all waste 30 minutes a day, and are paid an average of $10 per hour each, the annual cost to the company will be $24,000.

A survey conducted in the United States by Robert Half Personnel Agencies, Inc., New York, showed the typical employee wastes about 3 hours, 45 minutes a week. For 1977 this added up to a total cost of $70 billion.

If employees *deliberately* waste time on the job, they are actually stealing from the employer. And time wasting probably costs business more each year than all other crimes put together.

Ways employees "steal" time from their employer include clock watching, frequent trips to the washroom, personal grooming, arriving late, leaving early, extended coffee breaks, personal 'phone calls and letters, correcting mistakes, taking unjustified sick days, extensive socializing, inattention to the job, reading magazines, novels, etc. on company time, operating a business on the side, and eating lunch at their desks and then going out for a lunch hour.

Smoking, in addition to being a health hazard, is also a time thief. According to a *Toronto Star* report (September 22, 1980) an average smoker wastes about one hour per day on the mechanics of smoking. And this doesn't include the time lost due to cigarette-linked illnesses. The report points out that Canada's 65 million smokers cost their employers about $200 million a year in absenteeism and reduced productivity. So add smoking to your list of employees' timewasters.

You can deal with deliberate time wastage the same way you deal with theft or insubordination, but not all time wastage is deliberate. Employees experience most of the time problems that plague their managers. Multiply *your* time problems by the number of employees in the organization and you've got a considerable cost in terms of poorly organized time.

It is estimated that the typical office worker is only 60-70 percent efficient. It is your responsibility as a manager to encourage employees to manage their time wisely. You can do this by setting a good example, making suggestions, and by encouraging employees to participate in time management programs.

To set a good example, you not only have to remain organized and time conscious yourself, you have to respect your employees' time as well.

Don't keep interrupting your staff throughout the day. Have a brief meeting with each of them early in the morning or late in the day and pass on all the assignments at once. Don't keep delegating if they're already overloaded, spread the tasks around. And be more interested in eliminating jobs than delegating them. Use this brief communications meeting to receive feedback, ideas, to juggle priorities, and plan the day. Leave a copy of your week's schedule with them. Tell them when you'll be away. Describe major projects you've got on the go. Tell them what important visitors are expected. Your employees are members of your team. And time management within a company requires team effort.

Don't keep your employees waiting while you finish "one more thing" or make "one more call." When they're in your office at your request, respect their time. When you make assignments be sure they have deadlines agreeable to both you and the delegatees. Don't be a perfectionist. Results are what you're after. Who cares if the i's aren't dotted or there's a typographical error in a report. Correct it by hand and send it out.

Continually make suggestions to your employees as to how they can save time and increase effectiveness. And make it obvious that you want them to make suggestions to *you* as well. Share ideas. Provide training. Make time management an ongoing program within your organization similar to those being conducted in the area of safety. Keep your employees time conscious. You'll reap the rewards.

How Your Secretary Can Help You

You may not *have* a secretary. But if you do, you'd better have a good one. A secretary can double your effectiveness or impede it. So make sure you develop your secretary to the extent that "secretary" is a misnomer. Administrative Assistant or Executive Assistant would be more appropriate for the one who: helps keep you organized; assists in decision-making; keeps low-priority material off your desk; accepts responsibility; anticipates your needs; shows initiative; creates; and plans. Your *assistant* is part of the management team and as such should participate in management development programs.

Don't settle for a typist, file clerk or receptionist. Develop a management assistant. Time invested here will be time well spent. In addition to the routine tasks such as filing and typing, here is what an assistant (secretary) should do for you:

1. Intercept routine mail, take appropriate action, reply to routine letters and send a copy of reply to you before filing.

2. Formulate replies to the more important correspondence and pass on to you for changes. Or gather necessary information to allow *you* to reply quickly.

3. Review minutes of all meetings, highlight those sections requiring your attention (using a yellow marker) and take action on those items not requiring your personal attention.

4. Screen all telephone calls and visitors. Handle everything possible without disturbing you. Pass on those messages requiring your attention to you, along with files or other information you may need in order to handle them.

5. Acknowledge all letters during your vacation or extended absence.

6. Arrange meetings and conferences on your behalf, including hotel arrangements, meeting notices, and follow-up.

7. Make all travel arrangements for you, includ-

ing transportation, hotel, car rental, and provide you with a detailed itinerary.

8. Maintain a follow-up system to ensure that action is initiated well in advance in preparation for meetings, trips, and major activities.

9. Keep watch on your time. Rescue you from visitors who overstay their time, non-productive meetings that go too long, and callers who won't get off the 'phone.

10. Participate in decision-making, planning, the organization of office furniture, inventory control, development of filing systems, and purchasing of equipment and supplies.

Review all time management systems with your assistant. Work together as a team. Hold stand-up meetings each morning to keep each other up to date. Encourage professional development. Pay well.

And your "time" will have a personal bodyguard.

CHAPTER 14

TIME MANAGEMENT
IN THE HOME

Take Good Work Habits Home With You

So far I've been discussing time management as it applies to our business-related activities. Yet at least 75 percent of our time is spent away from the job. We cannot expect to manage our lives by concerning ourselves with only work-related activities.

To be in control of our lives we must manage our time at home as well. That is, we must organize ourselves in our home environments in such a way that we spend as little time as possible on those necessary, yet unrewarding activities that keep us from achieving our personal goals.

Goals will be different for different people. Your goals may include spending more time with the family, taking an evening course in automotive repair, teaching your children how to cook, building a rec room, and jogging every evening—whatever is important, meaningful, and enjoyable to *you*. It's unlikely you derive much pleasure from searching through the 'phone book for telephone numbers, picking up after the children, searching for misplaced items, and running up and down the stairs. You may not even enjoy mowing the lawn, washing the dishes, talking on the telephone or entertaining guests.

You are the only one who can determine how you would like to spend your time. But once you have determined it, you can *do* it. By being organized.

You can adapt many of the systems used in the office to the home because many of the activities are similar. You constantly make and receive telephone calls. You write letters, pay bills, and file correspondence. You receive visitors. Delegate to family members. You read magazines and books. Schedule projects and tasks. Handle crises. Make decisions. Travel. Plan.

So just like the office, you should have some central place from which you operate: An office in the basement, a desk in the bedroom, a table in the den, or even a corner of the kitchen table. It should be a place where you can schedule the occasional quiet hour free from the blare of the T.V. and exuberant children; a place where you can reach the telephone, have space for a file box, writing materials and the usual small office supplies such as stapler, 3-hole punch, and paperclips; and a place for your personal organizer.

The personal organizer is similar to the daily organizer or planning binder described in Chapter 5. It will help keep you and your family organized. It will be your reference book for everything from emergency numbers to metric conversion tables. It will be a training manual for babysitters. In sum, an information center. It will be what you *want* it to be, depending upon what you put into it. One thing's certain—it will be a big timesaver.

In a 3-ring binder place two sections described in Chapter 5: a telephone and visitors log, and a directory for telephone numbers. Insist that your family use the log to enter all incoming calls and messages. Put a stop to forgotten calls or misplaced messages. And have *everyone* enter their friends' telephone numbers in the directory. So next time your son tells you he's going to John Wilson's, you'll know how to reach him. And the next time your daughter has to reach *you* at Aunt Ethel's, she'll know how to contact *you*.

Have a separate section for emergency numbers: police, ambulance, close relatives, fire department, doctor, and hospital. It will not only save time, it may sometime save a life.

Make up another section for emergency repair numbers: service station, motor league, furnace, air conditioner, television, and appliances. This and other sections will save a lot of searching through old records or through the telephone directory. Enter the repair service number at the time you buy the appliance.

Get plenty of dividers and mark the tabs clearly. The more sections, the faster you can locate the material. And there'll be no need to keep writing out detailed instructions every time you have a new babysitter. You can have a section labelled "Where It's At"—spare fuses, light bulbs, key to the garage, and extra bedding. Include a separate "Babysitter" section if you want, complete with standard instructions and necessary information. A section on restaurants will also be useful. List phone numbers and addresses of your favourite take-out restaurants. How about a "Household Hints" section where you can keep useful information you've collected on removing stains, metric conversions, and cooking charts.

The possibilities are unlimited. Make up the sections that will help keep you and your family organized and save time. If you find you have to look up certain numbers or search for certain information on a regular basis, include it in your binder. Birthdates, family records, monthly expenses—anything you have to refer to frequently.

Those items you don't have to refer to frequently but must be kept for future reference should be filed. A cardboard file box with hanging folders is ideal. It can be tucked away on the closet shelf. Label the tabs on the hanging files with broad categories such as "Finance", "Appliances", "House", "School", "Recreation". Use manila folders for more detailed breakdowns in each category: for example, "Finance" may contain folders marked "Bank Statements", "Stocks and Bonds", "Retirement Plan" . . . as many subcategories as necessary to allow you to retrieve a document or letter quickly.

Don't file for the sake of filing. Throw out everything unless you feel you'll have to refer to it again. If you have a category labelled "Credit Cards" which is broken down into the various cards such as American Express, The Bay, Sears, Visa etc., file your record of payments if you feel it necessary to check each monthly statement with the previous one. But if you pay on the basis of each statement without question, why bother? Your cancelled cheque is your proof of payment.

If you must file, you must also clean out your files on a regular basis. Don't allow fat files in your home. Set up a schedule and stick to it. If you pay your bills monthly, file and discard monthly as well. A tier of trays described in Chapter 2 can be used to accumulate mail. As it arrives, toss it into the appropriate tray. They can be labelled "Bills", "Correspondence", "Junk Mail", etc. You may want to discard junk mail daily, answer correspondence weekly, and pay bills monthly. If you get mail which must be acted on immediately, label the top tray "Urgent".

Use the wall calendar described in Chapter 4 to schedule those hundreds of important dates, activities, and chores that crop up during the year. Post it where the whole family can see it and use it.

Make sure everything is marked on the calendar as they become known—school holidays, vacations, club meetings, sports events, dentist appointments, and social events. You can even schedule major household chores on this calendar such as wallpapering that spare bedroom or fixing that leaky faucet. You may want to color-code the entries. But keep it simple.

Make up a checklist of all the regular monthly and annual chores and repairs, such things as car maintenance, cleaning furnace filters, lawn treatment, and fur storage. Add them to your wall calendar. It's a simple matter to copy these same activities on to next year's calendar. And the next. You will never have to forget anything again.

In addition to a family wall calendar you need a central message board. This can be a cork board, clipboard with note pad, or simply magnets and index cards on the fridge door. With active families, this communications center is necessary to conserve tempers as well as time.

Organize Your Home

In addition to organizing yourself, you must organize the home. Much time is wasted in the home by having to search for something only to find you don't have any left. Or running up and down the stairs. Or cleaning out the junk drawer. Or trying to locate a certain shirt, blouse or necklace. Or the hundreds of other useless activities caused by not having a place for everything and everything in its place.

A common complaint of most apartment dwellers *and* homeowners is that they don't have enough storage space. Give them ten times as much space and they'll still complain. For Parkinson's Law applies to personal and household articles as well—they expand to fill the space available. What you must do first is get rid of articles you don't need or use. Give them away. Donate them to charity. Sell them. But get rid of them. Then move the less frequently used items into semipermanent storage. This applies to everything: clothes, dishes, toys, jewelry, cooking utensils, and garden tools. For example, clean out your clothes closets. Anything you haven't used for a year or more, get rid of. Store the items you use only occasionally in a garment bag, suitably marked as to contents, and move to the basement, attic, utility room—anywhere out of the way. Prime space should be reserved for those items you use fequently. Pack those special dishes (that are so special you hardly use them) into cartons, and store them on a top shelf in some secluded place. Do the same thing with bedding, silverware, toys, kitchen utensils, small appliances, etc. Make sure every carton is marked as to contents. Make up a master list of where everything is stored. Keep it in that family binder discussed earlier. Soon you will find you have more room than you need.

Effectively utilize the space you do have. Build extra shelves in closets, racks for shoes, storage boxes on rollers for beneath the beds, cupboards to the ceiling in laundry room and utility room, shelves beneath the stairs, and hooks on the bottom of cupboard shelves. Store all your articles so they don't have to be stacked on top of one another, or shoved out of the way so they can't be seen. And have a place for everything.

One shelf or cupboard should be reserved for "spares"; that is, things that keep burning out such as fuses, light bulbs, batteries, faucet washers. Another shelf should contain only those items that keep being used up, such as toilet paper, hand soap, tissue paper, toothpaste, garbage bags, vacuum-cleaner bags, lunch bags, fondue fuel, and paper towels. Another shelf (in the laundry room) should hold only laundry supplies; another cupboard or shelf for emergency canned goods. And so on. Keep all these storage depots well stocked. Don't let yourself run out of anything. Buy frequently used items in bulk. Plan your purchases. You'll find you save at least two hours per week by not having to continually rush to the store for things you've run out of.

Store the items you use daily *in the area where they will be used*. Don't keep shoepolish in the basement if you shine your shoes in the laundry room. And don't keep ointment in the bathroom if you always burn yourself in the kitchen.

Your time does not change in value just because you're off the job. So don't squander it. Farm out jobs you don't enjoy doing. Buy labor-saving appliances and equipment. Have plenty of 'phone jacks and a long extension cord so you don't have to run from room to room to answer calls. Keep a "to do" list of jobs. Schedule the ones you want to or have to do yourself. Let those necessary trips (cleaners, shoe store, barber, shopping, bank, library, etc.) accumulate and accomplish them all with one trip to the plaza or mall. Arrange your trips so you hit the bank, supermarket, etc. when they're not busy. Plan ahead. Schedule. Keep organized. You'll have more time for doing what you really *enjoy* doing.

CHAPTER 15

MAKE TIME MANAGEMENT A WAY OF LIFE

Personal Organization

Watch organized people and see how they operate: there's very little hesitation, indecision, and confusion. No double takes. No frantic movements. No frequent searching. Very little wasted motion. They are smooth, calm, and seemingly unflappable. They are in control.

They reach for files confident that the item they want is there. They slide open a desk drawer, and retrieve a petty cash pad without fumbling or groping. They answer the 'phone unhurriedly while reaching for a pen and telephone log. They appear calm. Relaxed. Efficient.

And very effective. You have confidence in them. They have a calming effect on you. They're the kind of people you would like to do business with. You know they'll get the job done. On time. Accurately. With a minimum of fanfare. They exude both confidence and competence.

These people are organized. They are managing themselves effectively with respect to time. They don't waste time on trivial matters. They don't experience the same crisis twice. They plan. They schedule. They place deadlines on all activities. They don't procrastinate. Once they've scheduled a job for a certain time slot, they do it.

They operate the same way in their personal lives. They don't make panic trips to the corner store every night to replace out-of-stock items. They don't watch T.V. programs they don't enjoy, or waste time searching for their racquet every time they want to play tennis.

Their homes are neat, organized, and there is a place for everything. And everything is replaced in its appropriate spot when not in use. There are no boxes or barrels of miscellaneous items to dig into constantly in search of something. No tangles of skates, bicycles or ski equipment. No rags wrapped around leaky faucets. No piles of shoes in closets. No mail strewn on the table, counter or fridge.

These people are seldom resented. Sometimes envied. Always respected.

You can be one of these people. But you can't do it by simply reading this or any other book on time management. Nor by attending seminars. Time management is a life-long concern involving more than common sense or gimmicky techniques. It requires a strong desire to enhance personal growth and satisfaction, to make life and work more meaningful and more rewarding. And it involves a dedication to become more and more organized: to break bad habits, form new ones, and adopt new methods. It involves a continuing search for new ways to increase effectiveness by sharing ideas and experimenting. And above all, it requires self-control, self-discipline, and persistence.

It's difficult at first—as breaking bad habits and

forming new ones always is. But then the rewards start to snowball. It becomes easier and easier and the increase in effectiveness becomes greater and greater. It's at this point when friends and associates will remark, "How can you get so much accomplished? You don't even look busy!"

Busy-ness always disappears as effectiveness takes over.

Time For A "Time Log"

Although most people will tell you the place to start is with a time log, don't believe it. Where you start is with this book—at the beginning. Get rid of your backlog first. Get organized. Establish objectives. Plan. Schedule your activities. Establish timesaving methods and habits. Train your employees. Delegate. Manage yourself effectively with respect to time. Then and only then, will you be ready for a time log. If you attempt to keep a log on your time as a first step, you'll never get to step two. Who's got time to record where they're spending their time? Hell, most people don't have time to *do* the activities, let alone record them.

But once you're organized and you've saved big chunks of time, you have some breathing space. Now you can become more sophisticated in your time management and actually keep a log for two or three weeks. That's the beauty of sticking to an ongoing program of time management. The rewards become greater and greater and it becomes easier and easier to save even more time and become even more effective. It's like the old saying, "It takes money to make money." It takes time to make time. And now you've got it. So make more of it. Keep a log on your activities for a few weeks and see where your time is really going. Then take action to reduce the time being spent on non-productive, low-value activities.

I recommend the time log found in *Getting Things Done* by Edwin C. Bliss, published by Charles Scribner & Sons. It's simple, easy to use, and accurate enough for our purpose.

Under the "Activity" section, write in those activities you seem to be spending your time on throughout the day and week, items such as meetings, correspondence, and telephone.

If you are responsible for different functions, such as production control, quality control, and maintenance —write those headings in under the "Business Function" section. If you're in sales, use this section to list your clients. Expand it if you need more room. You can even use it to list the employees reporting to you. The purpose of a meaningful time log should be to (1) tell you how much time, on average, you are spending on the various activities, and (2) tell you which functions, departments, clients, employees etc. you are performing these activities for. Then you are able to evaluate your time allocation. It's one thing to spend two hours per day on the telephone, but even more revealing if most of that time is being spent talking to a client or customer who accounts for less than one percent of your sales. Remember, you want to spend the majority of your time on the important, high pay-off activities.

Keep a few dozen sheets on a clipboard and leave it to one side of your desk. Every hour or so, check off the time spent on the activities you've listed—round off to the nearest 15 minutes to coincide with the time intervals on the log. It takes only seconds to check off the appropriate number of spaces. Yours should be different.

Keep it up for at least two weeks. Then transfer the totals to a fresh form.

Examine the results. Ask yourself questions. Are you spending more time on meetings than you realized? How can you reduce this time? Can you delegate some of the activities you're still doing? Are you happy with the amount of idle time, personal time, and travel time? How can it be reduced? Are you spending time in areas that bring you minimum benefit in terms of personal and organizational objectives? Are low-paying customers monopolizing your time? Ask as many questions as the results bring to mind. Take action. Be stingy with your time. It's your life you're spending. Be sure you get something valuable in return.

There's No Ending

Time management is not a finite skill or a body of knowledge that can be studied for 2 days, 2 weeks or 2 years, learned and then put into practice. Like time itself, it is never ending. It is a continuing process of managing yourself more and more effectively with respect to time.

Search out ideas, new methods, new techniques, and adapt them to your use. Investigate timesaving products. Wage a campaign against bad habits which rob you of precious time. Form new habits. Keep your goals in mind—*and* on paper—and refer to them constantly. Review them. Revise them. Make sure everything you do relates to them. For the purpose of managing yourself with respect to time is to achieve these goals. If you have no goals, you have no need to manage yourself with respect to time.

Review this book again. Take out any ideas that might

help you. Put them into practice. Stick to it. If there's no way these suggestions can apply to your particular situation, fine. But be honest. Try everything possible. In time you may find that almost all the checkmarks are in the "I do this now" column.

But don't stop there. Time management is neither an art nor a skill. It's a way of life.

You *can* control what you do and what you accomplish in the time you have left.

Do it.